S0-BMV-193

"For all who want their hearts stirred, Linda has gathered a smorgasbord of wonderful stories proving romance can be more than a wish—it can be a reality."

—Claudia Arp, coauthor of *10 Great Dates* and *The Second Half of Marriage*

"Linda Evans Shepherd's *Heart-Stirring Stories of Romance* will delight you, inspire you, and warm your heart—enjoyable, entertaining, creatively written stories that demonstrate that truly 'the greatest of these is love'!"

—Cheri Fuller, speaker and author of two dozen books, including the best-selling *When Mothers Pray* and Gold-Medallion award winner *Extraordinary Kids*

"After reading *Heart-Stirring Stories of Romance*, I've come to the conclusion that, not only does God love romance, but he gets the same big chuckle out of arranging romantic circumstances as we mere mortals get when we retell our stories!"

—Nancy Kennedy, author of *Honey, They're Playing Our Song* and *Prayers God Always Answers*

"Romance. Intrigue. Unexpected encounters. Unforgettable proposals. Tearful good-byes. Heart-lifting reunions. Love and laughter. Linda Evans Shepherd has skillfully woven a series of romantic stories into an inspiring volume that you will not be able to put down. I laughed out loud and wiped a few tears as my heart was captured by this delightful compilation of stories. If you have ever longed to read short stories that will lift you out of your current circumstances and give your mind a rest while inspiring your soul, this is the book for you!"

—Carol Kent, speaker and author of *Becoming a Woman of Influence*

"All women love a good romance, the happily ever-after. Through *Heart-Stirring Stories of Romance*, readers get the reality of lives lived together, the joy of working them out, and the happily ever-after, all stirred together to create a book that will warm your heart and lift your spirit."

—Marita Littauer, president of CLASServices, Inc., speaker, and author of *Personality Puzzle* and *Getting Along with Almost Anybody*

"If you like a good love story (and who doesn't?), you're in for a treat! Linda Evans Shepherd's delightful potpourri of true romances speaks to the heart of everyone who's ever loved."

—Karen O'Connor, speaker and author of thirty-five books, including *Basket of Blessings: 31 Days to a More Grateful Heart*

"These life sharings are an awesome encouragement for the foundation of family, celebrated and worked out in love."

—Naomi Rhode, CSP, CPAE, past president of the National Speaker's Association, Cavette Award winner, and author of *The Gift of Family* and *More Beautiful Than Diamonds*

Heart-Stirring STORIES OF Romance

LINDA EVANS SHEPHERD

BROADMAN
&HOLMAN
PUBLISHERS

Nashville, Tennessee

© 2000 by Linda Evans Shepherd
All rights reserved
Printed in the United States of America

0-8054-1972-1

Published by Broadman & Holman Publishers,
Nashville, Tennessee
Acquisitions & Development Editor: Vicki Crumpton
Text Design: Sandman Creative Group, Nashville
Typesetting: Leslie Joslin, Gray, Tennessee

Dewey Decimal Classification: 248.8
Subject Heading: ROMANCE
Library of Congress Card Catalog Number: 99-15101

Scripture quotations marked NASB are from the New American Standard Bible, © the Lockman Foundation, 1960, 1962, 1963, 1968, 1971, 1972, 1973, 1975, 1977, used by permission; NIV, the Holy Bible, New International Version, © 1973, 1978, 1984 by International Bible Society; and TLB, The Living Bible, © Tyndale House Publishers, Wheaton, Ill., 1971, used by permission.

Library of Congress Cataloging-in-Publication Data
Heart-stirring stories of romance / compiled by
    Linda Evans Shepherd.
            p.   cm.
        ISBN 0-8054-1972-1
        1. Spouses—Religious life. 2. Love—Religious aspects—Christianity. I. Shepherd, Linda E., 1957–.
BV4596.M3H43   2000
248.8'44—dc21
                                            99-15101
                                                CIP

1 2 3 4 5 04 03 02 01 00

To my husband Paul—
I have found true happiness with you.
Thank you for your love and encouragement.
I love you.
Linda

Contents

My Heart Stirred with Romance

There is no instinct like that of the heart.

Lord Byron

When I was first approached to write a book on romance, my first reaction was, "Don't the editors realize I'm married to a 'just-the-facts' computer engineer?"

Yes, Paul and I love each other, but flowers and heart-shaped boxes of chocolate are not an everyday occurrence in our home. Which may be a good thing since I have hayfever and we both hope to refrain from shopping for that "next-size-up" at the department store.

But then I realized how much love, trust, and respect Paul and I have invested in our twenty years of married life.

As I thought back on our own marriage stories, I realized, "Yes, I do have a wonderful tale of romance to tell."

In the pages of this book, you will have the chance to read our story, plus you will read the incredible stories I have collected from romantics around the country. The bonus for you is that these stories will teach you to not only *long* for romance, but will show you how to *live* it.

I want to give a special thanks to all those who wrote to share their stirring stories of romance with me. You made me laugh and cry, and you helped me treasure my own husband just a little bit more.

So, dear readers, pull out a tissue, pour that cup of coffee, and get ready to reach new heights of romantic joy!

Linda Evans Shepherd

1
Blossoms of Romance

We can only learn to love by loving.

Iris Murdouch

The Greatest of These

Nanette Thorsen-Snipes

My day began on a decidedly sour note when I saw my six-year-old wrestling with a limb of my azalea bush. By the time I got outside, he'd broken it. "Can I take this to school today?" he asked. With a wave of my hand, I sent him on. I turned my back so he wouldn't see the tears gathering in my eyes. I loved that azalea bush. I touched the broken limb to say silently, *I'm sorry.*

I wish I could have said that to my husband earlier, but I'd been angry. The washing machine had leaked on my brand-new linoleum—if he'd just fixed it the night before instead of playing checkers with Jonathan. *What are his priorities, anyway?* I wondered. I was still wiping up the mess on the floor when Jonathan followed me into the kitchen. "What's for breakfast, Mom?"

I opened the empty refrigerator. "Not cereal," I said, watching the sides of his mouth drop. "How about toast and jelly?" I smeared the toast with jelly and set it in front of him. *Why was I so angry?* I tossed my husband's dishes into the sudsy water. Days like this made me want to quit. I just wanted to drive my car up into the mountains, hide in a crevice, and never come down.

Somehow, I managed to lug the wet clothes to the laundromat. I spent most of the day washing and drying clothes and thinking of how love had disappeared in my life. Staring at the graffiti on the walls, I felt as wrung out as the clothes left in the washers.

As I finished hanging up the last of my husband's shirts, I looked at the clock on the wall.

Two-thirty. I was late. Jonathan's class let out at 2:15. I dumped my clothes in the back seat and hurriedly drove to the school. I was out of breath by the time I knocked on the teacher's door. I peered in through the glass. With one finger, she motioned for me to wait. She said something to Jonathan and handed him and the two other children crayons and a sheet of paper.

What now? I thought, as she rustled through the door and took me aside. "I want to talk to you about Jonathan," she said.

I prepared myself for the worst. Nothing would have surprised me. I had had a fight with my husband and we weren't speaking, my son had broken a limb off my favorite bush, and now this. "Did you know Jonathan brought flowers to school today?" she asked. I nodded, trying to keep the hurt in my eyes from showing. I glanced at my son busily coloring a picture. His wavy hair was too long and flopped just beneath his brow.

He pushed it away with the back of his hand. His eyes burst with blue as he admired his handiwork. "Let me tell you about yesterday," the teacher insisted. "See that little girl?" I watched the rosy-cheeked child laugh and point to a colorful picture taped to the wall. I nodded. "Well, yesterday she was almost hysterical. Her mother and father are going through a nasty divorce. Tish said she didn't want to live; she wished she could die. I watched that child bury her face in her hands and say loud enough for the class to hear,

'Nobody loves me.' I did all I could to console her, but it only made matters worse."

"I thought you wanted to talk to me about Jonathan," I said. "I do," she said, touching the sleeve of my blouse. "This morning, your son came straight for Tish. I watched him hand her the flowers and whisper, 'I love you, Tish.'" I felt my heart swell with pride for what my son had done. I smiled at the teacher. "Thank you," I said, reaching for Jonathan's hand, "you've made my day." Later that evening, I began pulling weeds from around my lopsided azalea bush. As I let my mind wander back to the love Jonathan showed that little girl, a verse from the Bible leapt at me: "*And now these three remain: faith, hope, and love. But the greatest of these is love*" (1 Cor. 13:13 NIV).

My son knew what God had said and had put it into practice. But all day I only thought of how angry I was. I dropped my head and whispered, "Forgive me, Lord."

I heard the familiar squeak of my husband's truck's brakes as he pulled into the drive. I snapped a small limb bristling with hot pink azaleas off the bush. I felt the seed of love that God planted in my family beginning to bloom once again in me.

My husband's eyes widened in surprise as I handed him the flowers. "I love you," I said.

The Color of Love

Vickey Banks

If love were a color, what would it be? I envisioned deep, fiery reds or soft, cotton-candy pinks, that is, until I sat on a hard hospital bed to talk with my friend, Annie.

Annie hadn't felt well for a very long time now. Looking upon her face last week, I saw the colorless lines of pain. Her uncovered arms were covered with bruises, a palette of yellows, grays, blacks, and blues. We were talking when she suddenly cried out and her hands grasped toward a shooting pain in her left leg. It was then that I saw her fingernails. Ten perfectly painted purple nails.

When the pain subsided, Annie saw me gazing at her hands. "Do you like my fingernails?" she asked. "Mark did them for me."

I thought of her husband, Mark, and of the relentless schedule he had been keeping. I thought of the weariness I'd heard in his voice lately and the exhausted look in his eyes. I shook my head and smiled at the thought of him sitting next to the same hospital bed I was sitting on, tenderly taking his wife's hands in his and lovingly painting her fingernails. No, he didn't paint away her pain, but he did color it with love.

If love were a color, what would it be? From now on, I will always think of it as purple.

It's Not Just in Movies

Denise Hawkins Camp

Single and living on my own, I spent Christmas day with my family and came away feeling discouraged. I wanted to fall in love, get married, and raise a family like my parents did. The trouble was, most guys I knew wanted sex and no strings attached. I wanted romance and commitment.

Everyone claimed marriage was a meaningless act and only slavery for women. My friends thought I was crazy. They thought I needed to be building a career that would be mine after a man left. Judging by the number of divorces, I wondered if they were right. No one seemed to care about building a life together as husband and wife.

My car broke down when I was out of town, and I was forced to stay overnight with friends. Their buddy, Dave, whom I barely knew, was giving a New Year's Eve party and needed an official date. I reluctantly agreed, although I was not in a party mood.

As midnight approached, a movie I'd never seen before, *It's a Wonderful Life,* was on television, and a group of us started to watch it. Someone said, "They don't make movies like this anymore."

Dave sat with his arm around me, and I actually caught a tear in his eye. I gave him a second look, and that's when our romance began.

Dave told me he loved me before I left town to go back home. We were married six months later. We refused to accept anything less than marriage.

Despite the warnings of our generation and even our parents' doubts that a whirlwind romance could make it, there hasn't been a day of regret during our twenty years together. Every New Year's Eve we watch the movie and look at each other and know that we truly have a wonderful life.

A Thousand Ways

Susan Titus Osborn

God has a thousand ways where I can see not one,
When all my means have reached their end,
Then His have just begun.

—*Esther Guyot*

Heavy snows were falling outside of Dick Osborn's parents' home in Boise, Idaho. He sat quietly in his room thinking about a dating relationship that had ended. Reaching for his Bible, he read, "We toss the coin, but it is the Lord who controls the decision" (Prov. 16:33 TLB).

Normally Dick wasn't the type to give God an ultimatum, but this particular evening he felt lonely and depressed as he thought about Sandy. He reached in his pocket for a quarter and flipped it up in the air, saying, "Lord, if it comes down heads, I will marry Sandy. If it doesn't, I know that isn't your will." The coin landed with the tails side up.

"No Lord, that's not the right answer. Let's go two out of three." He tossed the coin into the air again, and it came down tails. The same thing happened the fourth time. "Well, this is just a bunch of hokey anyway," he said.

Glancing around the room, Dick's gaze fell on a *Lookout* magazine lying upside down on the rug. On the back was an advertisement for the book *Parables for Young Teens*. Dick stared at the book's picture and read the author's name. He pleaded, "Lord, who am I going to marry—Susan F. Titus?" He flipped his coin up in the air again, and this time it came down heads.

"Well, that just proves that this is a bunch of hokey. I don't even know anyone named Susan F. Titus. I don't even know what state she lives in. How could I possibly marry her?" He soon forgot the incident.

While attending a church group, I met Dick. We were sitting around in a group, laughing and talking, and I said, "The thing I miss most from my previous marriage is the baseball tickets to the California Angels."

Dick said, "It happens, Susan, that I've got season tickets to a box seat. Maybe we can go sometime."

I whispered discretely, "I'd like to, but I'm dating someone."

Dick smiled and responded glibly, "Let me know if you ever change your mind."

Several months later, Dick was shocked to find out that his old girlfriend, Sandy, was engaged. The following Sunday he walked with me from the church sanctuary to the parking lot. I stopped and said, "Dick."

"Yeah?"

"Remember what you said about my telling you if I ever wanted to go out with you?"

"Yeah!"

"Well, I'd like to."

A smile lit his face. "OK."

We had lunch the following Wednesday. It didn't take long before we became engaged. One day, while Dick was carrying some of my son's things upstairs to his room, he noticed a framed poster hanging on the hall wall that read, *Parables for Young Teens,* authored by Susan F. Titus.

He stared open-mouthed, then turned to me, "Did you write that book?"

"Yes," I answered. "Why else would I have it hanging on my wall?"

He didn't respond but just stared at me incredulously.

While we were on our honeymoon, he told me the whole story. He squeezed my hand and laughed. "But you'd better not tell anyone. I don't think they'd ever believe it."

2
Prayer of Romance

Wither thou goest,
I will go; and where thou lodgest,
I will lodge: thy people shall be my people,
and thy God my God.

Ruth 1:16 KJV

The Lost Ring

by Lydia Hall as told to Beverly Caruso

I went to Samoa as a bride of only two weeks. As Youth with a Mission leaders, Dave and I cherished our times alone together. About eight months after our wedding, we went to the beach near the village of Fagalele. From the shade of a coconut tree, I watched Dave snorkel.

After several hours of relaxation, we packed up our gear and headed home. When we reached the pickup truck, I noticed Dave's wedding ring wasn't on his finger and asked him about it. Our rings were a matching set, with a tiny cross of diamonds on each one. We knew that finding a lost ring was unlikely in the pounding surf, the coral, shells, and sand. But we at least had to look.

After about thirty minutes, we gave up and drove home with sad hearts. We struggled with the loss of this small, yet precious token of our love for one another. We knew it was only symbolic, that a ring doesn't keep a marriage strong, but it seemed that God wanted to teach us something new about surrender.

Two weeks later, we returned to the same beach with other young people. I kept thinking, *Somewhere in that big Pacific Ocean is Dave's ring. Only God knows exactly where.*

After the guys snorkeled for about an hour, Dave brought me a handful of pretty seashells. Secretly I wished it were his ring that I was admiring. Then he brought his other hand forward. In it lay his wedding ring! He said that all the guys had looked for the ring for over an hour. At last they gave up. He told me he prayed that if God wanted the ring to be found to please put it right in front of his eyes.

Just before he got out of the water, Dave saw a pretty shell and reached below the water's surface to pick it up. While putting the shell in his pocket, his eyes seemed glued to what his mind was having difficulty believing. Just as he had prayed, the ring was right before his eyes—underneath the shell he had picked up!

Now the ring has been given to Dave twice, once from me and again from God.

From Darkness to Light

Marlene Bagnull

Unemployed! It had been nine years since we had faced that dismal situation. We had believed it would never happen to us again.

As the days stretched into weeks, the reality of being unemployed threatened to overwhelm us. Unemployment checks didn't stretch far enough to pay all the bills, put food on the table, and provide everything our two children needed. The cost of providing our own health insurance was staggering. Our savings account was dwindling more rapidly than we had anticipated. Furthermore, we were living with the uncertainty of not knowing how long Paul would be out of work. Some days it was more than we could handle.

Deep within we knew God was in control. For six months we had been hoping to move to North Carolina, but Paul had only one interview in all that time. Two days after Paul was laid off, he received three calls about jobs right in the area we wanted to move.

We made the trip. Paul interviewed for all three jobs, and we found exactly the home we always had dreamed of owning. Even so, we still had many questions and doubts. *Will Paul be offered one of the jobs? Will our home even sell in time?* It seemed unlikely.

The realtor's visit didn't help. By the time he had gone from one end of the house to the other, we were convinced we had a white elephant no one would want to purchase. Everywhere we looked, something needed to be repaired. We didn't know where to begin, but friends kept assuring us that a fresh coat of paint would work wonders, so we decided to start with that.

"We've probably got paint in the basement we can use," Paul said.

Together we went down to the basement and started hunting, but it was difficult to find the paint because the basement's fluorescent tubes kept flickering. *The same as my faith,* I thought to myself.

Remembering that the Bible teaches us to pray about all things, we stood there and began to pray.

"Oh God, please let there be light," my husband prayed.

"Yes, Lord," I agreed. "We can't keep walking in this darkness."

The light continued to flicker. Paul's shoulders slumped as he turned and took the cans of paint out to his workshop to pry open the lids. It was probably more stubbornness than faith, but I continued to stand under the flickering light, asking God to give us his light.

Gradually my petitions changed to praises. "Thank you, God, thank you that we know you will not allow us to walk in continual darkness."

The fluorescent tubes suddenly shone brilliantly, and light flooded the basement. I let out a squeal of joy as Paul came running.

"It's a sign from God," I wept. "He's going to get us through this."

Paul wrapped his arms around me, and together we thanked the Lord for his light and for the promise that no darkness will be able to extinguish it.

You've Got Mail

Barb Loftus Boswell

When asked, I often tell people that my husband, Brian, and I met "through a mutual friend." This is actually an oversimplification of things but not entirely an untruth. Actually, we met on an Internet website called "Christian Connections."

God is the "mutual friend" of whom I speak! As Brian says, with his somewhat off-center wit, "If God could once use a donkey to speak in his behalf, he can certainly use a computer!"

Before I met Brian, I gave my sorry-excuse-for-a-love-life over to the Lord. I had been trying to make romance happen all on my own and had quite a "Hall of Shame" to boast for it! I finally stopped, prayed, and allowed God to take control.

Enter the Internet. I was only browsing when I came upon the Christian Connections website. It never crossed my mind that this would be the avenue where I'd find "true love!" My expectation was to perhaps make a few new friends, but I found much more than that! I found Brian.

At first Brian and I wrote to each other; then we exchanged phone numbers. Finally, one night, he suggested we meet in person.

Meet in person? I was nervous! I had become quite fond of Brian over the weeks of letter and telephone exchanges; we shared a love of books, music, and most importantly, the Lord. In fact, he told me how he had handed his love life over to God about the same time I did!

But to meet in person? What if we disliked the sight of each other instantly? I can honestly say that I did a great deal of introspection and praying over it, but I didn't know if I could totally disregard appearance if Brian was not my idea of handsome.

When the fateful day arrived, my mom cautioned, "Just be careful."

I prayed over and over, "Please, God, just let him be attractive to me and me to him!"

The doorbell rang, and I peeked around the door and found the sweetest smile I had ever seen! I didn't tell him until after we were engaged, but I knew instantly that we would spend our lives together!

Now that we are married, the romance continues. Nothing is beyond God's reach! Our "mutual friend" had brought us together!

First Kiss
(aka Bowled Over)
Jan Coleman

"I know it's the last minute," Carl said when I answered the phone, "but I, um, need a date for tonight."

A date? Carl had never once mentioned the "D" word to me before, and it left me speechless.

"I hope you're available," he added.

It was after four. How many other numbers had he dialed first? "It's my company party—a bowling party," he said.

Bowling? He needs a date for bowling?

After I told him I'd go, I thought back two years before, when Carl first joined our church singles group. Something about him attracted me; his strength of character. Here was a man who had stayed faithful to his first marriage, a man who honored God, a man I could trust.

After the singles meetings, we were often the last ones at the coffee shop, talking until late into the night. I was like a soggy piece of toast, gazing longingly at him, but got only congenial smiles in return.

Every week my heart fluttered at his warm hello. He must be attracted to me, too, but this guy guards his heart like a sentry over the crown jewels.

A few months later at our group's annual country hoedown, Carl and I square danced together most of the night, twirling, tripping, and laughing like teenagers.

He offered to drive me home after we cleaned up. "I have a view of the valley from my deck," I said, nudging Carl through the front door to the backyard. "Come and see."

As we stood close together, watching the city lights flicker, I thought my anxious heart was about to explode like a pan of sizzling popcorn. This is the perfect moment for him to sweep me into his arms. Then, abruptly, he said, "I've really got to go now."

"He's driving me crazy," I later told my best friend Jeanne.

"Could you be misinterpreting his attentions just a bit, Jan?"

"But, but . . ." I was about to counter with, "He likes to be with me, and we have so much in common, and doesn't he realize I'm perfect for him?!!" I took a deep breath, *What was the matter with me?*

I was a mature, professional woman and a singles group leader, not a schoolgirl dizzy with her first crush.

Jeanne piped in. "Earth to Jan—remember that seminar on dating God's way? Remember the 'I' word?"

Infatuation, the chemistry that turns the sensible into silly. Yes, and it's the mystery, the uncertainty, that keeps the fires of infatuation going. Infatuation either turns into real love or it fades.

"I must be imagining things that just aren't there."

"You're in love with the idea of falling in love."

I suppressed some tears. "I feel like a fool."

"Let it go, Jan. It's not in God's timing right now," Jeanne said.

She was right. If Carl were the right man for me, it would happen without plotting on my part. During prayer, the Lord pressed on my heart, *Do you care about Carl enough to want the best for him, even if it is never you?*

I wrestled with it all night. *Yes, Lord, but how is it possible to have a platonic relationship while this medley of feelings dances on my heart?*

"Give your feelings to God," Jeanne had said.

Letting go was so hard but not as hard as trying to spark a romance with only one flame.

In the next year, Carl was in singles heyday. He had his share of women chasing him. He did have some dates, but none with me. Finally content to be his pal and front-line cheerleader, my life went back to normal.

Then came the telephone call. I raked over my closet, hoping to find the perfect bowling outfit. *Oh, here I go again, feeling all giddy.* I took a deep breath. *After all this time? Get a grip, girl.*

We met for dinner at a Mexican restaurant near the bowling lanes, and before the fajitas stopped sizzling, the atmosphere shifted. This was not our usual, "Let's grab a bite to eat."

This was a lingering meal. His eyes were riveted on me, soaking in my every word as if he'd never seen me before. This was a real date! And to clinch it, he paid for my dinner!

While I didn't make any strikes later at the bowling alley, there were telltale twinkles in his eyes that showed me I'd made a big strike with him. Bowled over, my emotional alarm clock started to go off.

Jeanne was half asleep when she picked up the phone at midnight. "What are you so afraid of?"

"That old floating-on-a-cloud feeling. I don't want to go back there."

"I like you better sane, myself."

Three weeks went by, and no telephone call from Carl. *It figures. He's probably back at Garcia's sampling the chile rellenos with somebody else. That's fine. At least I got a nice dinner out of it.*

It was time for our Saturday social—a trip to San Francisco, a bike ride in Golden Gate Park, and an optional dinner cruise on the bay. We rendezvoused at the grocery store parking lot.

When Carl showed up and began unloading his bike from the back of his car, I bolstered myself up. *Be mildly sociable but aloof. Let him come to you.*

After biking along the beachfront, several of us boarded a blue and gold double-decker boat. As it headed out in the choppy waters, we all stood on the lower deck, watching the blazing sun slip under the Golden Gate Bridge coloring the sky like a dream. I was spellbound by the lights emerging from the bridge. I barely noticed the music starting to signal dinner being served.

I saw Jeanne and the group go below, and suddenly the deck was empty, except for Carl and me.

As the boat began to circle, a cold blast of sea breeze made me shiver. Carl slid his long arms around my shoulders. This was no benign hug. Suddenly I froze like a petrified tree. Gently, he lifted my chin and looked down at me. *He's going to kiss me! In the most romantic place in the world, he's going to kiss me. Wait a minute. I have a few questions . . .*

I closed my eyes, slipped my arms around his neck, and just let it happen.

"I knew you wanted me to do that long ago," he finally said, "but I wasn't ready for a committed relationship, and it wouldn't have been right. I needed time to become the right man for a woman like you."

Eleven months later we were married. During our wedding vows, Carl said, "Thank you for waiting for me, Jan."

When it was my turn, I shared something I'd tucked away in my heart. It was from that dating seminar. *Love is a friendship that has caught fire.*

I Believe!

Linda Evans Shepherd

"If you go out with Paul Shepherd, I'll never speak to you again!" my friend, Ellen, warned me on the telephone.

I twirled my long brown hair around a finger. "Go out with Paul? I don't even know him," I insisted, thinking of the handsome, dark-haired young man I had met in the tennis shop with Ellen that night. His blue eyes had perked with interest when he saw us. "I'm just closing up shop," he had told us. "Let's go cruise Eleventh Street."

I had graduated from high school two weeks earlier and had just started to date. But I was cautious. As I meekly crawled into the backseat of Paul's red Nova, I couldn't believe I was getting into a car with a strange guy to go cruising. *But Ellen knows him,* I decided. *He must be all right.*

As we drove up and down the street, Ellen sat in the front seat and chatted away, but I never spoke a word.

Now I could hear Ellen's anger on the phone. "Yes," she reminded me, "but you've gone out with two other guys I introduced you to. This time, I want Paul for myself!"

"Don't worry, I promise I won't go out with Paul," I pledged. "Besides, he never even noticed me tonight."

Seconds after we hung up, the phone rang.

A lively male voice announced, "Hi, this is Paul. I met you at Ann's Tennis Racket tonight. I called and got Ellen to give me your phone number."

I caught my breath. "Have you been trying to call me the last few minutes?"

"Yeah, but your line's been busy."

My eyebrows shot up. *That Ellen!*

Paul continued, "I wondered if you'd go out with me?"

I gulped. Maybe Ellen had set me up, but still, I had given her my word.

I bit my lip. "Well, I don't know," I stalled. "I really don't know anything about you."

"That's OK," Paul said. "I'm playing in a tennis match Saturday afternoon at the college near your house, I can just swing by to see you afterwards. I'll call you first, OK?"

"OK." I can turn him down when he calls me, I thought, feeling somewhat relieved.

Later in the week, another charming young man asked me, "Will you go out with me Saturday night?"

That will get me off the hook with Paul and Ellen! I thought as I gladly accepted Allen's invitation. *I can tell Paul I have another date when he calls.*

Paul's call never came. *He must have changed his mind after all,* I reasoned.

Saturday evening, a few minutes before my date with Allen, Paul pulled his red Nova into my driveway. Being a mature seventeen-year-old, I panicked. What was I going to do with two dates?! I shrieked the situation to my mom and ran to my closet in my bedroom and slammed the door. I could feel my heart thumping as my mother told Paul, "Linda's not here."

Paul drove away just as Allen pulled his red Nova into our driveway.

Before Allen rang the doorbell, my mother popped open my closet door. Her green eyes snapped as she said, "Don't you ever put me in that position again!"

"I won't," I promised, still trembling with alarm. I was only a novice at dating and was already in over my head!

Even after all the confusion, Paul continued to call me. However, I refused his dating invitations even though Ellen was now seeing someone else.

"You're not a believer," I explained. "My faith is very important to me. I don't want a dating relationship with someone who doesn't understand me on that level."

Paul was baffled. He had never been turned down for a date before. He told me he would check into this "faith thing."

After that, he continued to call me regularly. The conversation always turned to explanations of God's love and grace. Paul was an agnostic, however, and he felt that maybe there was a God and maybe not. He wanted proof before he would believe.

That fall, Paul left for school at McNeese State University in Louisiana to study physics. I remained behind and began my studies in communications as a freshman at Lamar University.

Paul continued to call from time to time to chat. As our friendship grew, I found myself being drawn to his stimulating conversations. I confided to my friends that if Paul were to ever become a believer, I was afraid we'd end up married!

One day I packed my bags for a Baptist student rally, Freedom 76, in San Antonio.

When I opened the door to my hotel room, the phone was ringing. I sat my suitcase down on the end of the bed and grabbed the receiver.

"Hi, do you know who this is?" asked the voice on the other end of the line.

"No, unless you came up with our group from Lamar. I don't know anyone in San Antonio," I said.

After much teasing, Paul admitted, "This is Paul! I'm here with the kids from the Baptist Student Union at McNeese. I saw your name on the hotel register and decided to call you."

I couldn't believe it! What better place for Paul to find faith! My roomies and I began to pray that Paul would finally come to an understanding with God.

Every evening, despite the fact that thousands of young people were attending the rally, my roomies and I would run into Paul at the various local restaurants. On our last night in town, my friends and I once again ran into Paul at a pancake house. When we sat at his booth, he told us, "I've finally figured out what Christians have!" His eyes twinkled.

My heart skipped a beat. "What's that?"

"Friendship!" he gushed.

My heart sank. We tried once more to explain, but nothing we said seemed to get through. He had been exposed to messages about God's love for a whole weekend, and still he didn't believe.

I was barely able to endure the ride to our hotel before the tears began to flow. I slowly climbed the stairs to my room. Feeling a presence behind me, I walked into my room, fell across the bed, and began to sob.

What I hadn't realized was that my door stood wide open. My buddies from Lamar saw me weeping and barged right in. "What's wrong?" my forty concerned friends wanted to know.

I couldn't respond. My roomies had to tell them about Paul, while I just sobbed. Everyone in the room began to pray for Paul to come to grace with God. We prayed for what seemed like hours. Finally, at about 11:00 P.M., the spirit of peace flooded my soul. My sobs ceased, and the prayers subsided as my friends slowly left the room.

The next morning I went down to put my luggage on the bus. Paul and his Taiwanese roommate, Supot, were hanging out in the parking lot. My face was so swollen from crying the night before that I was embarrassed to be seen.

"Did Paul tell you he's a Christian now?" Supot asked when I approached the pair.

I turned to look up at Paul in surprise. "What's this?"

Paul dug a tennis shoe into the pavement. "After you left," he admitted, "I had a long talk with Supot. He told me once more that Jesus died for my sins so he could forgive me. I decided there was either something to all this, or not. I decided to believe and accept God's forgiveness. I decided to make my commitment to follow Christ with everything I had."

Stunned almost beyond words, I asked, "What time did this happen?"

"About eleven last night."

"That's when I felt the peace!"

"What?"

"We were upstairs praying for you. We prayed until I felt the peace."

Paul turned to look at me with surprise.

As our eyes met, I felt my heart flutter. I didn't know that this was the start of something big, but I did know I was free to finally get to know Paul on a deeper level.

(To be continued . . .)

3
Dates with Romance

Now join your hands,
and with your hands your hearts.

William Shakespeare

A Good Man Is Hard to Find

Maxine Holmgren

How does a fifty-seven-year-old widow meet a nice, morally upright man her age? I'd tried going to dances. I don't know which was worse, fear of not being asked to dance by the right man, or fear of being asked to dance by the wrong man! My sore feet and I soon decided that dancing down the road to romance was not for me.

My next venture led me to go join an over-fifty singles group whose main activity was going for walks along the ocean beach and ending up at a coffee house. I developed a great tan and met some lovely husband-seeking women, but no men!

In desperation, I finally started reading the "personal" ads. Some sounded very interesting. I decided to take a chance and started to make phone calls. I would chat on the phone with a gentleman, and if he seemed like a "possibility," I'd agree to meet him for a day-time coffee or lunch. I met four or five men that way.

I am tall, and I soon discovered that men who said they were six feet tall always turned out to be about 5' 10". Some were nice; some were not so nice. When one of the men found out what I meant when I said I believed in "old-fashioned moral values," he told me that if I was not willing to sleep with a date, I had no business answering ads!

I met one man who seemed to be nice, but he seemed extremely nervous. His name was Mike, and he talked nonstop during our meeting. I barely got a word in as, on and on, he spoke intensely.

As we said good-bye, I thought to myself, *I'll never see him again,* as he was obviously intimidated by me. He seemed glad the meeting was over as he hurried to his car.

A year later, I was still singing the good-man-is-hard-to-find blues. Then I discovered a Christian singles newsletter, and I placed an ad in it.

I soon received a call from a nice-sounding man who proceeded to leave a long message on my answering machine telling me all about himself. I immediately recognized him as the nervous nonstop talker, Mike. Just to be polite, I returned his call and said, "You know, I'm pretty sure we met a year ago."

Mike said, "Well, maybe the Lord has a reason for leading me to call you and have us connect again." So, we agreed to meet for lunch at a popular ocean-front restaurant that Sunday after church. I explained that I was involved in a church activity after church and might be a little late. Mike said he would wait.

Sunday came, and after church I hurried to the restaurant as fast as I could get away from my commitment. I searched the restaurant but couldn't find Mike. Had he stood me up? Did one of us have the date mixed up?

When I got home, I called him. He explained that he had been there, waited a while, then left, thinking I had stood him up! (Being stood up happens often to men, I discovered later.) So, we made another lunch date.

This time he picked me up, and we drove down the beautiful California coast. It was a warm, sunny day, so when we heard a popping noise and a sudden spray of water hit the windshield, I knew it wasn't rain but car trouble!

Mike turned the car around and nursed the over-heated engine back to town. We parked at the first place with a phone and tried to decide what to do. There seemed to be only one solution. Mike sheepishly called his son to come with his truck and tow the car home, and I called my daughter to come and get me.

Mike felt foolish about having to call our kids to get us out of trouble. (Hadn't we done the same for them just a few years ago?) They arrived shortly, each trying to hide grins from having to rescue their parents from a disastrous date.

Now, you might think that a relationship that started out as badly as that had no chance at all. But Mike and I both saw the humor in the situation and laughed about it.

In fact, we're still laughing about it, and we've been married for two years now!

A McDonald's Prom

Laurie Heron

"You can't go to prom this year. We just don't have the money." My dad's voice almost quavered as he made the announcement. He had recently lost his job, and he seemed ashamed that his failure had caused me so much grief.

I knew that "failure" didn't describe my father, and honestly, I felt little disappointment about the prospect of not attending my senior prom. I had gone to a formal ball, and it hadn't impressed me. High-school students got dressed in expensive, often unattractive clothing and spent a lot of money on unimportant things. Also, in my school, it had become the "in" thing for the girls to lose their virginity on prom night. I didn't need that kind of pressure. "It's OK, Dad. I didn't want to go anyway," I assured him.

Yet, as the day inched closer, I began to feel a twinge of regret. It *was* my senior prom. I successfully tossed the thought aside until the day I actually got invited.

Shane was the quiet type, and I had never realized he had any interest in me. I loved talking to and hanging out with him, but I had never considered him a prom date. When he asked, I sadly explained the situation to him, afraid that he might see it as a personal rejection.

He grinned. "Oh, I'm not talking about a regular prom date."

I knew Shane well enough to expect something interesting. "What are you talking about then?"

No amount of prying would entice him to explain further. "Just wear something pretty. I'm not going to rent a tuxedo. We'll just look as if we were going to a regular dance."

The intervening weeks passed more slowly than a car with my grandmother behind the wheel, but finally the night arrived. I could see the gratitude in my father's eyes when Shane came to pick me up, and I felt relief that he no longer had to bear his feelings of failure about this issue.

No flowers decorated our clothing, but I felt both secure and attractive. I didn't want to worry about ruining an expensive dress, even if I couldn't wear it more than once. We drove in silence. Shane seemed ready to burst with his surprise.

After driving a short distance, we pulled into the parking lot of a McDonald's. I couldn't help being disappointed with Shane's lack of imagination, but I certainly had no intention of complaining. My disappointment in Shane's choice of restaurants quickly changed to disappointment in myself for having doubted him. Shane opened the door for me then offered his arm to lead me to the table in the corner. Lighted candles sat atop a white linen tablecloth, and cloth napkins completed the elegant effect.

I couldn't believe how much effort Shane had made on my behalf, and I became even more amazed when his best friend brought our food, bowing deeply at the waist. "For the lady," he said in a phony French accent while he set the plate down with finesse. "And for the gentleman."

My night of surprises had not come to an end. Robert, Shane's fourteen-year-old brother, exhibited his musical talents for us. Customers stared at the table in the corner when Robert's violin began to sing.

I felt no embarrassment at being the center of attention. I just basked in the glow of Shane's thoughtfulness.

The rest of the night passed smoothly. Even my friends, who had gone to very expensive restaurants, seemed jealous of my experience. My senior prom night will forever remain a fond memory. Though I no longer see Shane, I always think of him when I hear the word *gentleman*.

Love's Night Out

S. F. Peacock

Searching through the many shelves of books, I soon found the first title on my list. Perhaps it was the smell of dusty old books or the sound of the librarian's voice when she told some young people to be quiet that caused me to stop my search. Standing there, in a narrow canyon of humanity's past ideas and thoughts, I found my thoughts flowing back some fifteen years to a time in my life when I made scheduled trips to the library with my husband.

We were young parents of three children and limited means. My husband worked long tough hours, and I spent equally long hours tending to our family and our home.

Weeks, which gradually led into months, would pass without a break in our routine. Our relationship as a couple began to come apart. I became crabby and he became sullen. There were no more off-to-work kisses or welcome-home smiles. The romance we once shared and enjoyed as young lovers had dimmed.

Living without romance was not what I wanted, so it was probably desperation that made me think of it. . . .

I arranged for a baby-sitter to arrive at 7:00 every Tuesday evening. No exceptions! It was our night on the town! *(Besides, it was dollar night at the theater!)*

If we did not want to see the movie, we would drive around town, take a short trip into the countryside, or share a booth, a burger, and a soda.

Above all else, we talked. We talked about what we did last week, about what we planned to do next week. We talked about the kids, schools, our church, families, friends, and our community. Tuesday evenings became our get-reacquainted night. These dates helped restore the electricity flowing between us.

The morning off-to-work kisses and the evening welcome-home smiles soon returned. Tuesdays ignited a steady flame of love between us, though it was not like a bonfire that suddenly glows bright and dies just as quickly. Instead, we enjoyed a constant burn, which supplied our marriage and family with an even and loving warmth.

The library? Yes, well, the library was one of our stops whenever the weather threatened, the movie did not interest us, or we did not wish to spend any money. We would sit next to each other on one of the couches and read magazines or page through travel books together. Yes, the librarian even told us to hush once or twice.

By the way, we gained one other benefit from our night out. In our home we had a rule: children were to be in bed and bedtime stories read by 8:30!

We never arrived home from our night out before 9:00. Would you?

Will You Go Out with Me?

Linda Evans Shepherd

(. . . continued.)

I was so glad that Paul was now a believer, and I couldn't help remembering the confidence I had shared with my girlfriends, "If that Paul Shepherd should ever become a believer, I'm afraid we'd end up married."

Since marriage was the last thing I had on my mind, I was glad Paul stayed with his tennis scholarship and physics studies at McNeese State in Louisiana, while I switched to art and drama studies at Lamar University in Beaumont, Texas.

At least we can keep a healthy distance! I hoped.

When the news came that Paul was transferring to Lamar, I fretted. *I've got to keep him at arms length. I don't want to fall in love!*

We did keep our distance. Paul and I dated others while continuing our friendship and nightly phone conversations.

One night Paul called me at home, "Are you going to be at the Christmas party tonight?" he asked.

"No," I said, as I leaned back in my white French provincial chair at my desk. "My sorority needs me to be at their Christmas party over at the house."

After I hung up, I sat on my rosebud bedspread, stared at the folds in my closed pink drapes, and thought about Paul's call. *I'm flattered he wanted to know if I'd be there,* I decided. *Maybe I should stop by the Baptist Union party and say, "Hi!" after all.*

Hurriedly, I dressed in my bright party clothes. When I rushed into the Baptist Student Union building,

I found Paul merrily sitting on the blue sofa with his arm around Alice, a pretty, blue-eyed blonde. When he saw me, he jumped and jerked his arm away. I noticed his response, and so did Alice.

"I thought you weren't coming!" Paul gushed as the crowd of partiers watched our exchange.

"I thought I'd drop by for a minute," I answered coyly. I waved to our friends, "Have fun without me. Merry Christmas, everyone!"

As I hopped into my Maverick, I thought, *So, Paul called because he wanted to be sure I wouldn't see him with Alice.* I grinned slyly. *Why should he care if I saw him with her? We're not dating.* I signaled my way out of the parking lot and pulled onto University Drive. *I know the answer to that question,* I thought smugly. *He's planning to ask me out!*

A few days later, I hosted a Christmas party at my home. Many of my friends came, including Paul and a young man named Richard. Richard was a shy student who often followed me around campus. He wasn't my type, but he was sweet. We sat in my living room playing board games and eating Christmas cookies as we visited with one another. All too soon, the evening turned into midnight. Most of my guests had left, that is, everyone except Richard and Paul.

I walked the guys to the front porch. The three of us stood under the yellow glow of the porch light and swatted mosquitoes in the balmy December air.

Shy Richard never said a word, while Paul and I talked nonstop.

Who will win this waiting game? I wondered, terribly curious.

Finally, when Paul realized that Richard was not about to give up, he stretched and stifled a yawn. "Well, Linda, I've got to get up early in the morning for church. I'll call you tomorrow."

"OK," I said as I waved good-bye. As soon as Paul headed for the front gate, Richard turned to leave too. When Paul saw Richard get into his car, he couldn't believe his eyes. He called back, "Wait, Linda, I forgot to tell you something."

Poor Richard stood in crestfallen defeat, as Paul, the victor, jogged back to my front porch. Still slapping mosquitoes, Paul and I waved good-bye to Richard's fading red taillights.

Paul turned back to me. "Would you go out with me next Friday?" he asked.

I gulped. I had tried so hard to avoid this moment. *If I say yes, Paul and I will end up married,* I realized. At nineteen I just wasn't ready for a serious relationship. I took a deep breath and looked up into his intense blue eyes, realizing that Paul had no way of knowing our dilemma.

I hesitated, then spoke firmly, "Yes, I will go out with you."

He smiled, and so did I.

Paul had no idea what he had set in motion that night when he asked me out, but I did. I knew this was the beginning of something that seemed to be God's doing. In my heart, I knew that Paul and I would someday wed. But I wouldn't tell him that then—it would have spoiled the surprise!

(To be continued . . .)

4
Heart-Melting Proposals

What is thine is mine, and all mine is thine.
Plautus

My Knight in Shining Levi's

Jan Northington

My day began like any other. I was a single mom of a three and a five-year-old, so I had already changed a wet bed, bathed and dressed kids, cleaned up spilled milk, and was now weeding in the backyard.

Suddenly, a voice interrupted my thoughts. "Jan, would you come out front? I want to show you something."

I followed my boyfriend's call and walked through the gate. There he stood holding the reins to a beautiful white horse.

Several months earlier I had admitted to him, "For the past two years I've put out carrots and sugar cubes every night waiting for my man on the white horse."

He announced with a grin, "I came by to take you for a ride. Hop on."

"My knight in shining Levi's!" I teased.

My heart pounding, we mounted the white horse together. As we rounded the street corner, he said, "Well, I guess you've figured it out by now. I did all this to ask you one question. Will you marry me?"

He expected me to say yes as we galloped toward the rocky shore to be silhouetted by the setting sun. Instead I stammered, "My answer is back home."

I could hear the disappointment in his voice. "You mean to tell me I'm proposing to you on a white horse and you don't have an answer for me?"

We galloped home, and I dismounted and ran into the house. There waiting for me was a banner I had made three weeks earlier. The children held one end while I unfurled its length across the front lawn. It read: MY ANSWER IS (PICK ONE) 1. DEFINITELY 2. WITHOUT A DOUBT 3. OF COURSE 4. CERTAINLY 5. ABSOLUTELY 6. ALL OF THE ABOVE.

Eight years have passed since my husband rode down Wilton Drive on a white horse and picked number six! Is there any wonder why I love to tell the story about the "prince" of my dreams?

The Gift of Honor

Naomi Rhode

From the very beginning of his dating relationship with Beth, Curt, who is now our son-in-law, always found a way to make our entire family an important part of their lives. When Curt asked our permission to marry Beth, we had no idea that Curt planned to make us an important part of his proposal.

During a family party, Curt pulled Jim aside and told him, "I have the ring, Dad, and I would like for you to give it to Beth."

What an incredible gift of honor! At the end of our meal, Curt, a deep-sea diver, pulled a seashell out of his pocket for Beth. She pulled a note out of the shell that read, "Will you marry me?"

Beth began to cry and passed the little note and shell around the family circle so that everyone could read it. Everyone was tearful, and as Jim handed Beth a napkin to wipe her eyes, he said, "You'd better look inside the napkin."

Much to her surprise, she found her engagement ring tucked inside.

Curt's gift of honor to Jim recognized the special bond of love between Jim and Beth. By presenting the diamond to Beth, Jim symbolized his approval of the marriage.

The Mysterious Proposal

Julie Moran Medearis

"Let's get together for a picnic," he invited.

When the day arrived, I pedaled my bicycle to his house, but he was not to be found. Instead, I discovered a map pinned to his front door. Puzzled, I grabbed it and set off to a familiar nature park.

"Why the map?" I mused aloud to my bike. "Why couldn't he have just waited for me?"

Once at the park, I pedaled up the steep, dirt hill. *What was going on? I suppose the chicken will be cold, and I'll look like a sweat hog after this hill!* By the time I'd crested the top and begun the downhill coast, I was feeling a little grumbly.

Midway down the hill, my boyfriend, trumpet in hand, jumped from behind an old oak tree and started playing our song! *How wonderful! If only I could stop.*

I finally wound my way back to him, realizing that his plans for the day included a beautiful concert in the park. Sweet and touching as this was, I still felt mystery hovering in the air.

Finally, under the cloak of California oak trees, my beloved knelt down, ring in hand, and proposed marriage to me!

How can I let this one go? I thought.

And now, ten years and three kids later, I still rejoice over that mystery's resolution. *What a proposal! What a man!*

47

Surprise Proposal

Jo Franz

"Hello," said a tall stranger with an engaging smile spreading beneath his dark mustache. Hazel eyes smiled down on me as he squinted in the bright sun's glare.

I didn't even catch his name before he held the cafeteria door open and we went our separate ways to sit with friends.

The following Sunday, my concentration on the pastor's sermon dissolved when I felt eyes boring holes through me from across the room. I peaked through the net of my black felt hat to see this same guy staring at me. During the refreshment break, he nonchalantly sat near me, and we chatted.

The following evening, as my friend Anne and I sat at the piano playing my newly composed songs, the phone's trill interrupted our thoughts as boldly as the newcomer's stares the prior morning. I made my way to the phone awkwardly, hanging onto chairs, the couch, then the walls.

"Hi, I'm Ray Franz."

"Um, could you describe yourself for me? I can't seem to place your name with your face," I said with embarrassment.

"I sat near you during the break at church." *Oh! The engaging stranger!* "I was wondering if you'd like to go to a movie and get to know me better."

After I offered to return Ray's call later when my friend left, I plopped down on the piano bench next to

Anne, saying, "I don't even know this guy! I don't go out with strangers, Anne!"

"It's not as if you can interview him first, Jo!" She laughed. Anne knew my concerns. She'd stood close by when my former husband of fifteen years divorced me following his affair with a girlfriend of mine. I was totally surprised when men later showed interest in me—not only because I felt so undesirable due to my unwanted divorce—but also because I had multiple sclerosis.

When I returned Ray's call, I indeed interviewed him—for forty-five minutes! Delightfully, I discovered we both enjoyed skiing, hiking, and biking. Yet, as I described the outriggers (short skis attached to crutches) I use for balance and breaking while skiing, the need to take rests while hiking, and the fun of riding a tandem bicycle, I voiced a concern to Ray. "You do know I have MS, don't you?"

"No, I didn't know that," he answered. I frowned. *This changes everything.*

After explaining multiple sclerosis to Ray, I discovered his good friend's wife had it. "She doesn't let it stop her either. You sound like you have a great outlook on life as active as you are."

Then I heard more intriguing information as Ray continued, "I've been raising my daughters by myself since my wife left me. It was a tragedy, but it gets easier over time. Lindsey was three, and Melissia was one and still in diapers. Everywhere I went I carried a diaper bag!" He laughed and so did I.

Despite how interesting Ray sounded to me, I offered him a graceful way out of the movie because he hadn't known about the MS. But he said, "I'd still like to go out with you."

During that first wonderful date we talked until one in the morning. I asked, "I'm curious. Why did you think I used the crutches? Most people ask."

"I didn't even notice them."

Surprised wasn't the word for what I thought. *Astounded* was more like it!

Our relationship blossomed quickly after that, from a young seedling to a steadily growing plant, with Lindsey, Melissia, and I loving each other at once. The girls enjoyed running up to me, spreading their arms until it looked like they would pop out of their shoulder sockets, then saying, "I love you thiiiiiiissss much!" Having these girls in my life along with Ray brought laughter, love, and glowing warmth. I hoped it would never end.

While awaiting Ray's nightly call on a chilly October evening, I lay on my bed, wrapped serenely in the comforter, reading my Bible. Ephesians 3:20 jumped out at me: "Now to him who is able to do immeasurably more than all we ask or imagine . . ." (NIV) with the promise of good things to come. Though I didn't know what God had planned, I thanked him as I picked up the phone receiver.

"Hi, how you doin'?" Ray's tenderness made me feel toasty inside and out.

"Good. I was just reading a great promise from God."

"Share it with me. But first, I need to let you know what I've decided about that job offer in California we talked and prayed about. It's such a good career move,

Jo, and I'd be close to my siblings. I need to try this," he explained. I knew he was right.

"I understand. Really. I want what is best for you." But as Ray continued to talk about his fear of commitment, a chill spread through me. It began in my heart and spread to my entire body.

What will this move do to us? I wondered. *No matter what, I believe God has given me this verse to claim.*

The painful journey of separation took all four of us through valleys of sadness and loneliness. The girls often called in tears, missing me. I cried in return, "We just have to trust God to work this together for good somehow. I love you so much. I pray for you all the time."

I poured myself into the speaking and singing ministry that gave my life purpose.

My friend, Ruth, prayed diligently for the relationship to be renewed. Months after his move, she called Ray and found out he missed me terribly and regretted losing what we'd been developing. This triggered the beginning of our long-distance relationship. We soon realized that during the separation God had obviously matured each of us through infusions of courage. The slow, steady drip, drip, drip of his love empowered Ray and me to believe someone could actually be trusted to remain committed. Our phone calls grew frequent. Longer. More expensive. We could hardly wait to see each other again.

In late June of 1987, I planned on filling Ruth in on Ray's latest phone call over my birthday lunch at the Gemini. I waited for her to pick me up. Finally the phone's ring disrupted my growing concern. "Ruth, is everything OK? Where are you?"

"Oh, I thought you were meeting me here. I'm sorry."

"It's OK. I'll be right there." I sped my Mazda immediately down Wadsworth Avenue toward the restaurant, weaving my way through traffic as quickly as I dared. I'm sure Ruth said she'd pick me up. What's going on? An odd sensation bounced around in my body and tingled my thoughts with anticipation. Something was up!

As I followed the maitre d' through the noonday crowd toward Ruth's table on the shaded patio, I saw her stand and wave. But she wasn't alone. Someone sitting next to her held up a newspaper as if deep in an article. *Who could that be? Why, I know those strong hairy arms! They're Ray's!* My heart pounded, my eyebrows raised, and my mouth dropped open.

I could see Ruth's grin. She looked like she'd just eaten a canary. The newspaper slowly lowered to reveal Ray's broad, engaging smile. When he stood up I rushed straight into his happy embrace. "You two!" I scolded.

The crowd around us clapped and cheered.

Ray and Ruth had cooked up the plan for him to fly into Denver and meet her at the restaurant, then for Ruth to call me. As she slipped giddily away from our table, Ray gave me a surprise birthday lunch I'll never forget. Women as well as men seated around us smiled and whispered. I glowed. Rich seafood crepes added to the glorious richness of the moment.

Following a lovely afternoon of lounging by my apartment's swimming pool together, sharing memories and dreams, Ray took me to one of our old favorites for dinner. Romantic Mariachi music played while sizzling fajitas wafted pungent scents into the air of Moosehill Cantina. We chose our favorite steaming chile rellenos with oozing cheese. As we toasted the evening with a tinkling of our glasses, I wondered, *Could life be more wonderful than this?*

Ray tenderly reached for my hand across the table. "I came to surprise you for your birthday, but I also want to ask you something." His thumb gently stroked the back of my hand.

Ray paused and gazed lovingly into my eyes. I thought I would melt into my plate of rellenos. "I know we've both been scared of commitment, but will you marry me?"

My eyes misted over as I squeezed Ray's hand. "I don't need to think about it. Yes!" I looked into his eyes, sparkling like mine with tears of joy, as he leaned over to kiss me.

Ray's surprise overwhelmingly proved how victorious God really was in the promise he had given me "to do immeasurably more than all we ask or imagine."

"I Will" in a Mud Hole

Doris Smalling

Rain flung its drops on the windshield as forcefully as Mom used to fling a large pan of water into the back-yard when the sink plugged again.

Duel, my boyfriend, peered intently through the waves of water washing over the car. *He hasn't mentioned the talk we're supposed to have tonight,* I realized. *Has he changed his mind? Maybe he's waiting until we stop for our after-the-show coffee and sandwich.*

"I don't think we better try to go to Jake's Coffee House, do you? It's raining too hard, and some of those drainage ditches probably overflowed the highway." *There goes our talk. Maybe it's not as important to him as I thought.*

"You're probably right." I didn't let him hear the disappointment in my voice. *Has he forgotten I'm supposed to give him an answer to his proposal tonight? Why am I feeling disappointment? I shouldn't. After all, I'm the one who said I wasn't sure I was ready for marriage again, though Ken died several years ago.*

I sat up straight, trying to see where we were. Duel's voice interrupted my reflections.

"I think we'll have to pull over. I can't see the sides of the road."

He tapped the brake. Suddenly—without warning—the car made a terrible grinding sound as if the bottom were being torn from the frame. It slammed forward instantly, tilting, rocking, front end down. I lurched forward. Duel threw his arm across me, protecting me from hurling into the dashboard.

"What on earth happened?" he asked. The car teetered. "Honey, are you all right?"

"Just a little shaken. Did we hit something?"

"I don't think so, but I'll get out and see if I can find out what happened. You stay here."

As he stepped from the car, it teetered, rocking back and forth. Duel opened the door.

"Listen, you'll never believe this. This street ends right here—no warning, no nothing. The car is suspended on the broken cement. It's like a teeter-totter."

"Will it go on over?"

"No, I don't think so, but the wheels and the front end are tipped down in mud clear up to the bumper. We're in a mess, and we're too far out of town to get help. Besides, there wouldn't be anything open to get help anyway. It's Thanksgiving Eve."

"What are you going to do?" I asked.

"I'm going to try lifting the front end, if the bumper holds. When I do, give it gas. It has rear-wheel drive, and we might get enough traction to make the back wheels catch."

How strong he is, and he's trusting me to do this right. Help me, Lord.

I gunned the motor. The back wheels spun furiously. I could hear them, but the car didn't move. I felt it drop again. Duel appeared at the window.

"I couldn't keep a grip on the bumper to lift it. I tried to use my suit jacket, but it's too soaked."

Duel opened the door and gave me a big kiss. He flashed the light in my face. "You, girlfriend, are a mess."

Playfully, I grabbed the flashlight and turned its light on him. "Oh, no," I squealed. We broke into laughter at his muddy appearance.

"I've got an idea," Duel suggested. "There might be some posts around here from the construction on that housing project over there. I can use it for a lever. Maybe that'll do the trick."

It seemed like ages before I saw his flashlight bobbing toward the car.

"I found one," he said. "I'll try to lift the front end so the wheels will hit the cement. You back the car the minute I raise it up."

Lord, please help us. Are you showing me he's patient under stress?

Almost as soon as he lifted the car, I hit the pedal. The car jerked fiercely as the front wheels grabbed the cement.

The car shot backward, taking me off guard. It jerked onto the cement so unexpectedly that I almost forgot to take my foot off the gas. I slammed on the brake, and Duel came running.

"I thought you were going to run off and leave me," he laughed as he slid into the driver's seat and I moved over. Water dripped from every part of him. Mud encased him from the waist down.

"We're going back to Main Street. It was clear when we came down earlier." *Still no mention of our talk.*

"One headlight's damaged, but I can get you home OK." I said nothing as we drove.

Unexpectedly, he pulled over under a street light and shut off the motor.

"I can't stand it any longer. I can't think of anything else. You said you'd tell me tonight what you wanted to do, but you haven't said a word. I've been afraid to mention it for fear you'll say no. Do you love me, or don't you? We're not leaving here until you tell me one way or the other."

"Oh, Honey." I laid my head on his wet chest. "I didn't think you cared because you never said a word about it all evening."

"Say yes or no, girl. Right now."

"Yes, Duel, yes! If I had any doubts at all, you sure got rid of them for me tonight. Any man who can act as calmly and patiently as you did must be a wonderful person, and that's what I want for a husband. Yes, I'll marry you."

He grabbed me in a crushing hug. "No more secrets from this point on. OK?"

"OK, you bet. Now we'd better go home."

As he started to pull away from the curb, he burst into laughter and slapped his hand on the wheel.

"I don't think I'll stick around to hear what your folks say when they see you. I think I'll run."

"Oh, no, you don't," I answered, joining in his laughter. "They'll never believe me unless they see you too."

A Change of Reservations

Beverly J. Anderson

Andy lived next door to me at the mobile home park where I moved when I started teaching in Concord, California. He and his wife became my good friends. She didn't get out much due to a mobility problem but loved to have company. She would often wave a coffee cup in the window when I drove in so I'd go over and spend time with them. Not long after she died, Andy said, "You know, the coffee is still hot. Come in, I need someone to talk with." So the habit continued.

Months went by. I dated several other men but found I could hardly wait for them to leave so I could go over and talk to Andy. We started going places together, and love blossomed. It seemed like we'd grown together gradually, and suddenly it was something different. However, I had reservations. He was much older than me, and I was even younger than his daughter. I'd lived just over half his years. Could something like this work?

I compared him to others I'd dated. He was more alive and more ready to try new things and discuss a variety of topics. Already retired, he was free to travel on school breaks. As much as I cared for him and felt comfortable in his presence, I decided it couldn't be. I'd pull back from the relationship. I even wrote a letter to tell him this just before I left to visit my parents who were wintering in Southern California's desert country. I did agree to let him take me to the airport and pick me up upon my return.

When I got to San Francisco, I found that the earlier commuter flight to Concord had room for me, so I took it.

People on the plane were talking about being met at the airport, and I had a twinge of regret that I wouldn't be. Then I thought, *I'll grab a taxi and surprise Andy. He'll see that I can take care of myself. We can be friends, but that's all.*

I carefully stepped down the stairs to the ground in the misty darkness.

Only a few commuter flights came in daily, and night illumination at the airport was minimal. I walked with the other passengers down the sidewalk toward the parking lot and small terminal. I'd not gone far before a hand grabbed my suitcase and the other was giving me a hug of welcome. "I was praying you'd have a safe flight and got this little nudging that I should meet the earlier flight, so I called for the arrival time. I'm so glad I did." Andy put the suitcase down next to his car for a hearty hug and more than a kiss of greeting.

My airline reservations were not the only ones changed. The hesitancy I had about our relationship developing further vanished. When the formal proposal came, I said, "Yes!" We knew we didn't have a quantity of years, so we went for quality. We were married nearly fifteen great years before he went to his heavenly home. I've never regretted that God stepped into the relationship to make things happen for the best for both of us.

Popping the Question

Linda Evans Shepherd

(continued . . .)

Paul was a college senior at Lamar. I was a junior. It had never occurred to me that he was ready to ask me to be his wife until one afternoon when I was driving my schoolbus-yellow Maverick to the library.

When the thought occurred, it stunned me. I shook my head. *No, he wouldn't ask just yet! Besides, it's only a week before my twentieth birthday. If he's planning to ask me soon, he'll at least wait until then.*

I relaxed. *I've got at least another whole week to think about it.*

You see, I was pretty proud of the fact that I was able to spot "that look" in a young man's eyes.

Busy with college activities, I had always side-stepped those lovelorn men who began to send out signals that they were ready to find a wife.

That's not where I am, I thought. *I'm having too much fun. There'll be time for that after I graduate.*

So, I was unprepared for the conversation Paul and I had that night.

We were snuggled together on my mom's ivory and green floral sofa in the living room. Paul turned to me. "I've been thinking . . . I'm going to be an engineer. That will be a dull, tedious lifestyle. I need someone like you who will add personality and fun to my life. I love you, Linda. Will you marry me?"

For once in my life I was speechless. Yes, I loved Paul too. That wasn't the snag; it was just that I had not yet come to terms with the only response I knew I would give.

"I can't tell you just yet," I stammered.

The hurt in Paul's eyes went straight to my heart. "I love you," I told him. "I just need time to think."

A week later, a very nervous Paul got down on one knee on the seafoam-green carpet to ask me again. This time I sat on the sofa and was prepared to answer.

Just then the phone rang and my mom called from the next room, "Linda, it's Jodie Ann. She wants to talk to you."

In those days before answering machines, I automatically lunged for the phone. As my hand reached for the nearby receiver, Paul looked doleful. I told him, "I'll just tell her to call back."

I grabbed the phone and Jodie gushed, "Linda, I hear you're engaged!"

I looked deep into Paul's eyes. "No, not yet."

"What? But your mother told my mother!"

Uh oh. I should have known to keep my mouth shut.

But now I had to get off the phone! "Well . . . can I call you back?"

"Why won't you tell me now?" Jodie pleaded.

"I just can't talk!"

I could tell she was miffed, but I had to get back to business. With a quick good-bye, I hung up.

Paul took my hand in his. "Linda, I love you. I want you to be my wife. Will you marry me?"

I threw my arms around him and smothered him with kisses. "Yes, yes, yes!"

Several hours later, I returned Jodie's call. "He was in the middle of asking me to marry him when you called!" I explained.

"Oh!"

"I had to tell him before I told you."

Jodie laughed. "I see your point."

Well, Paul got through that proposal with a few hitches. But he was the one who wanted me to spice up his life. I'd say I've been holding my end of the bargain from the moment he asked! And as I've told him on many occasions, "At least you knew what you were in for."

(. . . to be continued)

5
Romantic "I Do's"

To have and to hold from this day forward,
for better, for worse, for richer, for poorer,
in sickness, and in health, to love and to cherish,
till death us do part.

Book of Common Prayer

An "IV" League Thanksgiving

Bonnie Compton Hanson

Fragrant pies baked in the oven. Cranberry relish chilled in the refrigerator. I was just getting ready to thaw the turkey—when the call came.

"Hello," I heard. "I'm from the County Hospital. Can your husband perform a wedding here tomorrow afternoon?"

As I sputtered for a reply, he explained. A young male patient had been injured critically, and he and his fiancée wanted to be married immediately. "Unfortunately, he can't get out of bed, they don't have a license, and they're broke. Can you help us out?"

On Thanksgiving Day? No way! But my husband was enthusiastic. So were my sons.

"If the wedding's at one," they reasoned, "we should be back home by two.

Instead of turkey, we could have something simple to eat and still have plenty of time for ourselves."

So much to do! Finally we arrived in our patient's room with synthesizer, flowers—the whole works. Surprise! Our groom was up in a wheelchair.

"It's a miracle!" his nurses cried. Then they told us the whole romantic story.

The young man had commuted fifty miles for his first day in a new job. Outside his new workplace, he'd been mugged, robbed, and left for dead.

Found unconscious by the police, he had been rushed to this hospital. But since his identification had been stolen, no one knew who he was.

His new employer wrote him off as a "no-show." When he finally came out of his coma and understood how critical his injuries were, he wrote himself off as well. "No girl would want to be burdened with me now," he reasoned.

Meanwhile, his desperate fiancée checked out every police station and hospital for miles around. Finally locating him, she convinced him that she still loved him, bedridden or not. That's when they asked to be married "on Thanksgiving Day because we are both so thankful to God to have each other."

What a wedding! A bride in white, a groom in IVs, and enough love to touch everyone watching—including a hallway of teary-eyed nurses and us as well.

Yes, I still missed fixing my traditional turkey. But we ate our sandwiches and pie with true love and thankfulness that day. And no feast ever tasted better.

God Listens

DiAnn G. Mills

"God, if you ever want a man in my life, you will have to put him there.

"In fact, he will have to be standing at my front door wearing a tee shirt that says so." Those words, spoken from bitterness and disappointment for the crushed relationships in my life, stated exactly how I felt.

Years passed, and my busy life centered around church, my four sons, and my job. My parents lived out of state, so our church became our family.

I slowly turned all of my joys, heartaches, and triumphs over to God.

During those healing years, my youngest son established a friendship with a man who assisted our youth music minister. Jack was a quiet, somber man who lived a life modeled after our Lord. He urged young people to find their identity through God's unfailing love. I admired Jack's patience, understanding, and giving ways. Most of all, however, I appreciated his friendship with my sons.

At first I felt suspicious of his spending time and effort on my sons, and I researched his background to ensure my sons' safety and well being. He received glowing reports for his integrity and devotion to God. I decided he had been sent to fill the void in my sons' lives and to be the role model they so desperately needed.

Over the next year and a half, Jack spent more and more time with my sons.

He took the youngest to Cancun during Christmas break one year, and shortly after he took two of them to Branson, Missouri. He purchased one of the boys a car so he could take a part-time job. Jack showed him how to pay for gas and insurance and still have spending money. He listened to my sons' escapades and problems and never judged or condemned their behavior. He just encouraged them to have a relationship with our Lord. He and I were great friends. I felt no threat to my sons or myself because Jack was twelve years younger than me.

One summer day the doorbell rang. Jack stood in the doorway wearing a tee shirt with the logo "God Listens." At that moment I remembered the words I uttered years before. I felt the color rise to my cheeks, and my stomach knotted. He handed me four additional shirts with the same "God Listens" logo printed on the front.

"I got these at the Christian bookstore, and there's one for each of you," he said.

All I could think of was, *Oh no, Lord, not Jack. He's not the right one. He's too young, and he's . . . well, he's my friend.* Naturally I said nothing, but thereafter the "God Listens" logo haunted me. I attempted to rationalize the entire incident, but God did not let me put the matter aside.

Two months later, Jack proposed. I had asked God to handle the matter for me, and he did. The boys were excited, and I suddenly realized how happy our lives had become since Jack had come into our lives. Still, I felt nervous and fearful of being hurt again.

Jack and I talked a great deal about a Christian marriage and the value of open communication. We made a budget, attended premarital classes, prayed together, and talked about our future.

We planned to marry in one of the church offices. Neither of us had family nearby, so we only intended for my sons and a few close friends to attend the ceremony.

We scheduled the wedding for ten o'clock on a November morning. Shortly before nine-thirty, the boys and I drove to the church office. One of Jack's friends waited outside to video the whole thing.

Once inside, I was amazed at the number of friends who had come to share in our vows. My best friend, my sons, and I stayed in an empty office while a photographer snapped various poses of us all. Of course, the video rolled on.

Promptly at ten, the pastor stepped in and announced that it was time for the wedding. We walked down the hallway to find even more friends waiting— but Jack did not stand among them.

The pastor reached inside his suit pocket and produced a folded piece of paper. "Jack could not be with us this morning, but he did leave a letter for Lisa," he announced.

A hush fell over the room, and I teetered between hysterics and sheer bewilderment. Why couldn't the pastor have pulled me aside to break the news? I stood in total humiliation and disappointment while my heart pounded furiously. Too stunned to even utter a protest, I watched in horror while he unfolded the letter. Suddenly, the thought of fainting held merit.

With heartfelt words, Jack began his letter by explaining how he had gradually fallen in love with each member of my family. He stated how his friendship with me had grown from admiration to a deep love. His first love was to Jesus Christ as his Lord and Savior, and he knew I shared the same feelings.

Together we would establish a loving, Christian marriage and realize the blessings of our Lord. His love and commitment extended to my sons as well.

Jack concluded the letter by stating that he was waiting for us at a secret destination and would meet me at the altar.

The pastor tucked the letter back inside his suit coat and escorted me to a church bus. I didn't know what to say for fear the lump in my throat would explode into a pool of tears. *Where could Jack be?*

We boarded a church bus with the video still filming my every emotion while I searched futilely for a possible wedding location. Each time I thought I knew where he intended to meet me, the bus drove right on by. We continued driving, and my mind raced with the possibilities. Then the bus turned into a lovely subdivision. Imagine my surprise to see that my husband-to-be had purchased a beautiful and spacious new home!

In the front yard, a sign leaned against a huge pine tree. It read: *The Mills Residence, established November 24, 1993.*

Inside, Jack and the pastor's wife had arranged candles, baskets of pink flowers, and a kneeling bench in front of a marble fireplace. In the dining room, I found a wedding cake and food for all of our friends. A black, grand piano filled our ears with the music of love. God had orchestrated a fairy-tale wedding, proof that God does listen.

The Wedding

Voni K. Harris

Am I doing the right thing?

The fearful thought shook Alexis as she and Jared stood before Pastor John and a hushed, expectant congregation. She anxiously smoothed her creamy white dress, careful not to damage her bouquet of twelve red roses, then smiled up at Jared. His tall, lanky frame was a dream on the basketball court. But standing there in his creamy white tux and red-rose boutonniere, Jared had his usual charming air of someone who didn't know quite what to do with his awkward elbows and knees.

Pastor John grinned at the couple, then began the service. "Ladies and gentlemen, we're not here to witness a wedding today. Oh don't worry. We will witness a wedding, yet there is much more going on than meets the eye. You see, man's love for a woman is symbolic of God's love for mankind."

Everything was fairy-tale perfect, except . . . *Am I doing the right thing?*

Alexis knew why the fearful thoughts were plaguing her as she felt the presence of her parents behind her. Mom in the front row. Father in the back row. They'd loved each other until Alexis was ten years old.

Then they divorced.

Am I doing the right thing?

Then, like rain through the desert, memories washed through her soul.

The first time she saw Jared, he was on stilts in the middle of the campus commons during the lunch hour. He simply wanted to try out some stilts, he told her later. In the tangle of stilts and legs and laughter after she accidentally dropped her load of books, she thought, *I've always wanted someone who could make me laugh.*

One day a few months later, she came barreling down the stairs of her dorm with her friends. He was standing there with a pizza. He grinned at her, "I've been looking for someone to share a pizza with." She gazed at Jared's square shoulders, tan face, and the lean power in his muscles. *I've always wanted someone who could take my breath away,* she thought as her friends went on without her.

I've always wanted someone who understood the deepest parts of me, she thought a few months later. She and Jared were sipping two long cups of coffee at Klatch's while she told him about how her parents' love died.

"Love isn't like that, Alexis," he said. "Love isn't a feeling. Feelings come and go, but true love is forever. Jesus Christ's love is forever." Her stomach knotted when he said that name . . . Jesus. But before that night was over, she gave her heart to that Jesus . . . love himself.

Jesus created Jared for me . . . mind, body, and spirit!

Jared's gentle elbow in her side brought her mind back to the wedding.

". . . I think you'll see from the vows Jared and Alexis have prepared for each other a glimpse of God's love for us symbolized through this young couple. You'll see how much Jesus means to Jared and Alexis and how much they mean to each other," Pastor John was saying. He invited them to begin, and Alexis hugged her sister as she handed her the roses.

Jared took her hands. Alexis looked into Jared's eyes, and what she saw there nearly made her forget her memorized vows. *God, let Jared see in my eyes the same powerful love I see in his.*

"Alexis, I trust God and I trust you with my past, my present, and my future, my life."

"Jared, I trust God and I trust you with my past, my present, my future, my life." Together they said, "Because God created us for one another, I pledge you my undying devotion, my unending faithfulness, my tender affections, and my love forever."

We've Got to get Married

Opal Ashenbrenner

"Here's a live one," Bob said. "Let's go visit him!" Bob and I were going through the visitor cards from church as we did every week after the Sunday worship service. We were looking for prospects for our single adult departments, a group that has about five women to every man. When we saw the prospect card filled out by a sixty-two-year-old man, we decided to check him out. We were not disappointed. He was no Tom Selleck, but he was attractive, clean, and as far as we could tell from one visit, in his right mind. As we left his home that night, Bob remarked, "You know, he seemed all right!"

"Yeah," I said, "if only I can keep him away from Velma Sue Higgins." Velma Sue is every single director's nightmare. She is an attractive sixty-something widow who lets every man fifteen years on either side of sixty know that she's available; has plenty of money, a nice home, a new car; and, is looking for a husband! Needless to say, most older men either came to our group only once or twice and ran as fast as they could in the other direction, or they accepted her offer, and the little affair ran its course. As singles director, I felt it was my duty to keep her away from this nice man. He would be an asset to our group if I could keep him coming.

The next few weeks proved to be a challenge. Velma Sue increased her efforts. She was determined, but I was just as determined. I began saving a place for Don to sit by me in the Sunday morning worship service. At every singles' activity, I made sure he was by my side at all times. Every time my back was turned, there she was. Don, being a typical male, didn't have a clue as to what was going on! He was just enjoying himself tremendously.

Finally, after almost a year, Velma Sue conceded defeat. She found a young man half her age and joined the married group at another church! The game was over!

What to do now? I wondered. *I'm beginning to like having him around.* By this time the entire congregation was looking at Don and me with knowing smiles.

"Lord," I accused, "you slipped one over on me, didn't you? I'm too old to think about falling in love."

When I resigned the singles director position, our friendship continued. I had no need now to sit by him just to keep someone away. I sat by him because I wanted to. We never spoke of marriage even though we both realized there was something special about our relationship. We both had been hurt too much to risk getting romantically involved. We just enjoyed being together.

Don was retired, and as an additional source of income, he bought HUD property to repair and sell. We enjoyed looking at houses together. I was his sounding board as he considered the possibilities of each house. I particularly liked one of the houses. However, two other potential buyers bid higher than Don. We continued to look at houses. Three months later the real estate agent called Don. "You've just bought a house, Don," the agent said. Don asked, "Which one?"

It was the house I liked. Neither of the two highest bidders had qualified for their loans. The house was

Don's by default. Don immediately called me. "Hey," he shouted, "we've got to get married; we have a house!"

That was not exactly the romantic proposal I would have expected. However, it worked! Even though we were sure of our love for each other by this time, there were many doubts. As we sought God's will, we felt his leadership in every plan we made.

With much fear and trembling, we set the wedding date. Our feelings ran the gamut from fear to excitement to joy. On our wedding day, an unusual calmness and sense of peace settled over the church as my daughter, Susie, began the service singing, "Sweet, Sweet Spirit." The candlelights and flower girls were perfect! Then it was time! The organist began the wedding march from the Sound of Music, and my heart beat just a little bit faster.

As I took my son-in-law's arm, he teased, "You can still back out, you know."

As I looked to the altar and saw my beloved standing there, I knew without a doubt that this was God's plan for Don and me. The sound of weeping filled the church. No one wept harder or longer than Don and me. God had given us another chance at happiness.

On a recent anniversary, I recalled the song Susie sang as we left the church six years earlier: "Only God Could Love Me More!" That's the way I feel today about Don, my companion, lover, best friend, and soul mate. Only God could have put us together at this time in our lives and allowed us so much happiness.

6
Heavenly Honeymoons

Happiness consists of living each day
as if it were the first day of your honeymoon
and the last day of your vacation.

Unknown

To Flee the Maitre d'

Linda Evans Shepherd

(. . . continued)

Paul and I were both the ripe old age of twenty-one when we married in my home church in Beaumont, Texas. Being poor, just-graduated-from-college types, we needed a cheap honeymoon. So we headed for the wilds of Galveston Island, the honeymoon capital of southeast Texas.

We didn't mind the confines of our tiny hotel room, and we enjoyed the beauty of strolling the sea wall to witness the rolling gray gulf and the deep blue sky. We also loved playing at the new super waterslide, which was located only a few blocks from our hotel.

The honeymoon was unmarred except for one detail. One evening, as the waiter seated us in a lovely sea-view window of an elegant restaurant, Paul stared at the prices on the menu. Suddenly, he grabbed my hand, and we ran for all we were worth—the stability of our financial future together.

Later, as we munched on hamburgers at a local fast-food stand, my face reddened over our embarrassing mad dash for freedom. But at the same time, I was glad to know that Paul was ready to protect our meager bank account.

Throughout our marriage, we have stayed in the black and enjoyed many meals in elegant restaurants. Though we no longer flee the maitre d', we remember our honeymoon with both laughter and joy.

Romantic Honeymoon

Ronica Stromberg

Before my husband and I married, we often teased each other about being old-fashioned. We recognized, unquestionably, that although we were in our twenties, we shared values from a bygone era. We both believed in God, maintained chastity before marriage, and treasured "the old"—family histories, antiques, and heirlooms. Beyond that, we treasured each other.

Just how much my husband, Lloyd, treasured me became clear to me the night of our wedding. He whisked me away from the dance floor and off to the mysterious destination he had reserved for this night but had kept secret from me for six whole months. He had chosen a Victorian bed and breakfast with beautiful antiques throughout our suite, a canopied bed with rose petals strewn across the sheets, and a bottle of iced champagne resting upon the nightstand. His thoughtfulness brought tears to my eyes.

Everything was perfect—until God made his sense of humor known. As we were preparing to consummate our love, we ran into a snag. We could not get the string that was holding up my hoop skirt untied. My personal attendant had tied the string firmly, and now, after a night of dancing, it held an unyielding knot.

Lloyd and I struggled with it for a time but finally had to give up. "What now?" he asked me. I shrugged and began searching the dressers for scissors. I wasn't having any luck and turned to tell Lloyd as much when

I noticed a merry, almost evil, glint in his eyes. He stepped toward me with a pocketknife poised in his hand. Here we were on our honeymoon half-clad, and he was approaching me with a lethal weapon! The absurdity of the situation struck us at the same time, and we broke into laughter.

The next day we left our honeymoon suite convinced we had experienced a honeymoon quite unlike any other—and all the more special for it. God had shown us that love truly does conquer all—even hoop skirts!

Love, Honor, and Trust Him?

Nancy Hoag

Married just over twenty-four hours, my husband and I began the first full day of our honeymoon in a sun-drenched, snow-covered, Rocky Mountain lodge.

It was a morning filled with both expectation and exasperation. Expectation, because on the downhill side of mid-life, I'd discovered love. Exasperation, because I'd married the leader of a national ski patrol team. A skier for nearly thirty years, my Montanan traversed the slopes more skillfully than most folks cut across dry land. I, on the other hand, couldn't tell one ski from another, let alone glide from the top of an incline to level ground. Furthermore, I'd spent most of my life trusting no one. Now this middle-aged bachelor had danced into my life, drawn me to his long lean frame, and exclaimed, "Trust me."

The agreement (before we were married) was that I'd never have to ski. "But I want to see you once in a while," I'd said. And it was obvious that five months out of every year he'd be skiing.

"It won't be that bad," my bachelor had said. "But, babe, it's up to you."

Up to me? Oh, sure. I'd seen the twinkle in his eye every time he mentioned deep powder.

The truth was, I could either take up tatting or learn how to deal with moguls and spills.

It took several weeks of wrestling, but once I had decided, there was no turning back.

"I'm skiing," I said, "and I don't care to discuss it again."

Now, however, as I drew the drapes and faced the mountain, I despaired. Equipped with the best gear (a wedding gift to myself), I had enrolled in ski school. While my spouse danced down Suicide Gulch with the ski patrollers, I'd stay on the bunny hill with twelve children barely three feet tall!

My husband is a kind and patient man. So, when I fussed aloud, slammed drawers, and refused breakfast, he just wrapped his arms around me and said, "Babe, you'll do great."

How could I resist such charm? I couldn't—so I donned the cumbersome clothing, shoved my hair up into a scratchy wool hat, and adjusted massive goggles.

Outside our room, wind-whipped snow bit into my face. I squeezed into my boots, then measured the incline and distance to the ski chalet.

"I can't do it," I wailed.

"Yes you can," Scotty said grinning. "I'll get you down that hill; it's easy. Trust me."

We may be husband and wife, I thought, *but he most definitely has a few more things to learn about me.*

This man's been skiing forever while I've spent years indoors. Trust him? I don't think I can!

As if he'd already read my thoughts, Scotty hugged me, chuckled good-naturedly, pointed to the class gathering below our room, and emphasized how short the distance would seem once I'd actually made it down the *slight* incline.

"Oh, all right," I said, "I'll do it."

The plan was to join forces, literally. Scotty explained that I'd stand behind him and slip my skis between his. He'd ski, I'd coast. I'd also press my face into his jacket, wrap my arms around his middle, and close my eyes.

"Close my eyes?" I screeched.

Again he smiled. Then he positioned my arms at his waist, patted my thinsulated hands, and shouted "Yahoo!" as he pushed off.

At first it wasn't so bad. In fact, I discovered I enjoyed skimming the snow—responsible for nothing—relying completely on someone else.

"This is kind of fun," I mumbled against my partner's broad back.

"What'd I tell you?" Scotty chuckled below his goggles, his words steaming in the air.

I returned the laughter, believing my trailblazer would get me safely to the bottom of the crusted descent.

We did occasionally encounter bumps along the trail, and I'd ask, "What was that?"—all the while trying to sound composed.

Scotty threw his head back and laughed, but I couldn't hear him because of the crackling ice and snow sprays. He patted my hands and said, "Don't worry; just hang on." And to my surprise, I did exactly as instructed.

However, nearing the bottom of the grade, we picked up speed.

Scotty had explained that we'd "accelerate a bit." But hearing him tell it and experiencing it suddenly seemed like two different things. I'd been given his promise that he wouldn't fail, but my skis were starting to part some and my old nature was beginning to deal with my new-born faith.

"How much farther?"

"We're doing great," my spouse assured. "Just relax."

Scotty's word meant absolutely nothing at this point. My fears and my evaluation of our chances had become all the proof I needed that we would crash and break every bone in our bodies. I froze.

"Relax!" Scotty shouted back over his shoulder.

"I can't," I cried.

"You've got to, babe! We're nearly there! Trust me!"

Scotty's assurance was no match for my doubt. Within seconds I'd not only begun to tip over, but I'd also thrown my spouse off balance. Four skis, three poles, one pair of goggles, and two prime-of-life bodies were suddenly rolling, slipping, sliding, and bouncing across an unrelenting, ice-covered knoll. Not three feet from our target, all my hopes and temporary pleasure had come to a painful end.

As quickly as a bruised man can, Scotty brushed the snow from his glasses, shook ice lumps from my hat, and questioned me about broken things while I tried to keep the tears from freezing on my face.

He said, "Babe, do you know what you did?"

I could only nod and sputter. Both my body and my pride had suffered, and I was certain I'd had all I could bear—until I heard my husband's "old buddies."

"Hey!" one ruddy-complexioned Norseman called as seven patrollers shot across the hill. "This must be the new bride!"

"She learning to ski?" another whooped.

"She sure is," Scotty laughed as he stood me upright again and pressed his lips to my wounded ear. He whispered, "And learning to trust too, right babe?"

"Right," I managed, feeling my husband's reassuring arms around me. I took a deep breath and smiled.

It was true. Despite the spill, I realized I was learning to trust. This "trusting-adventure" would prove to be the most exciting ride of my life.

Leaving Americana Bliss

Sheila Seifert

Except for breathing the smog in Los Angeles, I am not a gambling individual. Yet, from the moment I stepped off the plane into the third-world country, I knew my honeymoon would be filled with unknown risks.

It wasn't until the large U-boats holding torpedo practice along our beach gave me my first indication that I was at the mercy of a land in search of an enemy.

By midweek we had survived tainted meat, germ-infested waters, and never being able to get the good waiter, no matter where we sat. We had killed unrecognizable bugs, ignored vendors peering in our windows, and had finally received a small glass of freshly squeezed orange juice for only ten dollars. In an attempt at honesty, I told my new husband, "If we don't leave this tourist-trapped land today, I swear I'll divorce you tomorrow."

After we argued for some time, Glen put his foot down on a cockroach and said, "This is our honeymoon, and we're going to enjoy it whether we like it or not!" Although his was the final word, the silence that followed was miserable.

We were so new at being a couple that making up was difficult. I was hurt, certain that I had made the biggest mistake of my life by marrying Glen. I think our process of reconciliation began two days later when I heard my husband ask the front desk clerk for a taxi to take us to the airport.

I'll never forget the romantic lilt in his voice as he asked, "Could it be here in an hour?"

In that phrase, I saw all the exotic sunsets I needed to brighten an otherwise darkened honeymoon. As if to make my happiness complete, he looked deep into my eyes and began to hum the "Star-Spangled Banner."

An hour later we slid into the back seat of a primed cab. I felt shy, as if we were on our first date. I barely noticed that the driver neither turned his head to see if we were settled nor glanced in the rear-view mirror. He applied one foot to the gas and the other to the brake. I was concentrating on what I should say to Glen.

Jerking past the town's main restaurants, I let myself become distracted by the thought that all of the U.S.'s fast food would be at our disposal in a few short hours. We would once again be able to pick up a balanced American meal consisting of an equal amount of cookies in one hand and potato chips in the other. Our taxi continued ten, then fifteen, then twenty minutes out into the desert.

Necessity helped me begin our conversation. "Glen," I whispered, "How long did our ride take to the hotel?"

"Maybe fifteen or twenty minutes," he said. We looked at each other and were silent. I wondered how I had let broken expectations and circumstances stand in the way of being with my new husband.

The driver turned his head to catch a glimpse of the vulture circling high above us. At the forty-five-minute mark, his mugshot began to look like a photo on the evening news in which a nondescript announcer states, "If anyone has information leading to the where-abouts . . ."

Glen put his arm around my shoulders, and I cuddled close.

"I'm sorry," I said. He gave my shoulders a quick hug. We had had a good marriage.

"I should have listened to you," he said. I gave a nod of forgiveness and leaned into his arm.

I was in the process of contemplating eulogies when we arrived at the airport.

Overjoyed by the thought that we were alive to experience the frustrations and misunderstandings that all married couples are said to go through. Even the days at home recovering from food poisoning from the in-flight meal could not remove my joy.

Though our exotic vacation had been dreadful, I was sure that our pictures would represent us as having a wonderful time. With each passing year, we would believe the paper smiles and laugh at the comically softened stories of this day. In time we would probably have wished our children and grandchildren the same beautiful honeymoon we had had.

Looking back I realized that it had taken a traumatic situation to bring forgiveness and to clear the air between Glen and me. Today, my joy to be alive and even experience arguments with my handsome husband seemed like a gift from God. I can hardly wait for the rest of our lives together.

7
Romance and the Kids

The house of the heart is never full.

African Proverb

Something Told Me

Linda Evans Shepherd

(. . . continued)

After seven years of marriage, I had resigned myself to the fact that we had no children. We were both busy, young professionals. Paul was a motivated engineer, and I was a budding technical writer who was using my experience of being married to an engineer to help me in my job, interviewing engineers and translating their "Engineese" into English.

One evening over dinner, Paul turned to me and said, "I think it's time to have a baby."

I was floored. "But we can't," I insisted.

"Why not?"

"You haven't darkened the door of our church in two years. I don't want to have children if we can't go to church as a family."

My strong silent type was silent. Finally he said, "Just because I've been busy climbing mountains on the weekends doesn't mean my heart is not right with the Lord."

The next Sunday I knew that what he had told me was true. As Paul sat next to me during the church service, his hand slipped into mine. I smiled at him and he at me. That's when something told me he would soon be a new father.

Nine months later, he was! He was by my side when our beautiful daughter, Laura, was born. A few weeks later he stood beside me at the altar at our church. Laura, a Gerber-baby-look-alike, was dressed in a delicate gown of lace. How proudly we held her in our arms as we dedicated her to the Lord.

I looked up at my husband, Paul. In his eyes I saw his commitment and trust as he took his new role as father to heart. How thankful I was that we would parent this precious child under the umbrella of God's love.

Shake, Rattle, and Push?

Nancy Kennedy

I became a mother quite by surprise. I don't know how I missed the clues: the swollen breasts, the need for a revolving door on the bathroom at night, the hysterical sobbing when Barry brought home Extra Crispy chicken after I specifically asked for Original Recipe.

It wasn't until the day I went for my annual checkup (and to discuss my recent bout of indigestion) that the possibility of a baby even entered my mind.

"What do you think about babies?" the doctor asked from the rather personal side of the paper drape across my knees.

Babies? We occasionally talked about them with our friends in a generic sort of way ("You going to have any?" "Probably someday, I guess."), but no one actually owned one. I vaguely remembered my mom having two or three after I was born, and I distinctly remember flushing my youngest brother's cloth diaper down the toilet and jamming up the plumbing. Other than that, I'd never had any experience with a real live baby. Now it seemed that I was about to, and by the doctor's calculations, my experience would begin in approximately six months. To celebrate, I bought my unborn prodigy a little blue dress (covering both gender bases) and planned how I'd break the news to Barry.

After an afternoon of meticulous plotting, I had it planned down to the last detail. Barry would come in from work and find me awash in my estrogen-enhanced pregnant glow and nestled in my favorite easy chair while knitting teeny, tiny pink and blue booties. As always, he'd kiss me on top of my head and ask, "How was your day?" I'd smile and keep knitting. Then, when he'd ask about dinner, I'd smile even more and inform him: "Tonight's menu will be baby carrots, baby back ribs, and zwieback biscuits to teethe on for dessert."

I imagined Barry doing a double take, then asking, "Does this mean what I think it means?" Before I could answer, he'd whisk me off my feet and lift me high in the air. We'd both laugh—then cry—and dance around the room together singing, "We're having a baby! We're having a baby!"

Well, take away the easy chair, the teeny tiny booties, the carrots, the ribs, and top-of-the-head kiss. While you're at it, take away Barry lifting me high in the air, the laughing (and the crying), and the dancing too. Now you have the real story of how I broke the news of my pregnancy to my husband.

The real story goes like this: I burned the ribs and overboiled the carrots, so I had to make do with a half-pound of hamburger, a jar of sauerkraut, and leftover angel food cake. Not only that, Barry couldn't walk in on me knitting because: I can't knit, and I had the car—a rental car at that since ours was in the repair shop—and I had to pick him up.

I plotted a back-up plan while driving to the air force supply warehouse where Barry worked. He looked so cute in his green fatigue uniform and his blue baseball hat (the one that had been run over a few too many times by the ton-and-a-half truck he drove!)

As he swept the warehouse floor, I tried to think of something witty and/or endearing to say or do. Finally, I came up from behind and tapped him on the shoulder.

I was about to blurt out, "Hi, Daddy!" Instead, all I could say was: "I-I-I . . . um, um, um. The mechanic assured me that the windshield won't leak this time. It'll be ready for sure this afternoon." I followed him around the warehouse for a few seconds, trying to speak, but only swallowing air. Finally I blurted it out: "I'm um . . . I'm, *you know.*"

He *didn't* know. My pregnant glow had turned to sweat and dripped down my cheek. I tried again. "Barry, I'm—"

"You're not." He threw down the broom he was using and turned to face me. "How did this happen?" he demanded to know.

I gulped. This was not in the script.

"Didn't you deposit that check I gave you?" he continued.

"Yeah, last week, but—"

"But nothing! How could you be overdrawn again?"

"Barry, I'm not overdrawn. I'm pregnant!"

This time it was his turn to stammer. He hugged me until I thought I'd squish. Then he squawked out, "I can't believe it! I can't believe it!" He asked his supervisor for the rest of the day off so we could go off to digest the news that one plus one was about to equal three.

The next day was our first anniversary. We just knew we were the first people on earth to ever have a first anniversary and a first baby on the way. We drove to the coastal town of Bar Harbor, Maine, to celebrate. We ate lobster and corn on the cob, then went back to our hotel room to do what every young couple does on their first anniversary.

However, we had a problem. Since we were the first couple to ever have a first baby, we didn't know if marital bonding would shake up the baby's brains. Barry was the first to bring up the subject.

"What if we shouldn't be doing this?" He jumped off the bed where we had been kissing. Then he chewed on his thumbnail and paced the floor.

"Well, I know it's legal," I tried assuring him. My pregnancy hormones were also working overtime and assuring *me* that not only was it legal, it was also moral and God-ordained—and very much desired.

Still, we were the first couple to ever experience this dilemma, and it just might have been true that marital bonding does indeed shake up a baby's brains. We leafed through all the hotel literature but found nothing to confirm or refute our fears. (After all, we were the first.) We finally called the nearest obstetrician to inquire—hypothetically, of course—of *bonding's* brain-shaking potential. After a brief chuckle, the doctor prescribed that the two of us go directly to bed and remain there the entire weekend.

We'd never enjoyed following doctor's orders more.

After that, the pregnancy continued as described in all the books. My mood swung. My ankles swelled. I fell asleep in the ladies' room of the air force commissary and woke myself up with my snoring. I discovered that a pregnant belly makes a dandy snack tray and often used mine to hold bowls of ice cream, plates of cheese and crackers, and entire six-packs of soda as Barry and I watched TV late at night (saving us numerous trips to and from the kitchen).

We dreamed and planned for B-Day (Baby Day) to arrive. When it did, it took us completely by surprise.

I'd had a hard day. All I wanted to do was flop on the couch and watch television. But gravity—or whatever it is that tells your body, "It's time!"—won out. As I flopped, my water broke, which signaled the need for us to shut off the television and try to remember our names and the route to the hospital.

We remembered and made it there in time for a game of "Just Where Is That Doctor?" and six hours of one of us crying to go home and forget the whole thing.

And I wasn't feeling too hot either.

At the beginning of the seventh hour, the bowling ball decided to make its entrance into the world. That's about the time one of the baby's parents decided he felt faint. As the pushing parent strained to turn her body inside out, the faint-feeling parent announced he might do better out in the hall—to which the pushing parent responded with dangerous-sounding threats muttered through clenched teeth.

The faint parent stayed and watched the birth of his firstborn while facedown on the floor of the delivery room, a bottle of smelling salts at his side. It was not the stuff of novels or dreams, but when we held our much-wanted and already-loved daughter, time stood still, heaven rejoiced, and God smiled at the miracle he'd just performed.

After that, Barry and I sighed with relief.

The baby's brains had not been shaken after all.

Moonlight and Roses and Kids with Stuffed Noses

Rhonda Wheeler Stock

"How about going to bed early tonight?" my husband whispers in my ear.

I rinse the last supper dish and ask coyly, "What do you have in mind?"

"I want to carry you to bed and have my way with you," he says in a darn good Harrison Ford impression.

"I'll meet you in the bedroom." With a wink of the eye and a wiggle of the hips, I saunter out of the kitchen. The seductive ploy is sadly spoiled when I smash my toe on the door jamb and grunt in pain. Kate Capshaw helped Harrison Ford escape a doomed temple or something; I can barely make it out of my own kitchen.

I hustle the kids through homework and baths. "Skip math tonight," I advise. "That's what computers are for. No, you don't need soap; just a quick rinse will do. I read somewhere that a little dirt is good for your skin; it protects you from ultraviolet rays. Pick out a bedtime story, a short one. Bambi? How about a condensed version: Bambi lives, his mother doesn't, he wins the fight, they all live happily ever after. Except for his mother. No, I don't know why a deer is king of the forest if a lion is king of the jungle. Yes, Bambi's a boy even though he has a girl's name. Let's say our prayers. There we go. Into bed. Hug, hug, kiss, kiss. I love you too. And you. And you. And you. Good-night.

"Good-night. Good-night. Good-night." I'm glad I only have four kids, I think.

Finally the kids are tucked away and the lights are out. I head toward the boudoir where I slip into something slinky. At least it used to slink. Now it kind of snugs. *Oh well.* I brush my teeth and comb my hair, dab my best perfume behind my ears, turn off the lamp, and light some candles. With the comforter turned down invitingly, I arrange myself in a glamorous pose among the pillows. I ignore the Snoopy pillowcase beside me; my bed linens have not matched since the Reagan era.

The door opens. In a throaty voice, I say, "I've been waiting for you, big boy."

"I can't sleep," a tiny voice whimpers.

Whoops. "What's wrong, honey?" I ask as I scramble into my robe.

"My tummy hurts. And my head. Can I sleep in your room?"

"No." I take Michael's little hand and lead him back to bed.

"You smell good, Mommy."

"Thank you." I tuck the covers securely. Would it be child abuse to nail the blankets down so they sort of immobilize him? Only temporarily, of course.

"Why are there candles in your room, Mommy?"

"Because she and Daddy want to smooch, that's why," says Josh, with all the worldly wisdom of a twelve-year-old boy.

"Good-night." More hugs, more kisses.

Back in my bedroom, I shrug off the robe and climb back into bed.

I settle against the pillows just as a yawn splits open my skull. "Those kids better go to sleep, and Rick better come to bed fast," I mutter.

"Mo-o-om," someone calls.

"What?" I bellow. Did Kate bellow at Harrison?

"Josh's arm is hanging down."

I grab my robe and stomp to the boys' room.

"What's wrong with his arm hanging down?" I demand.

"It's bugging me," says Jason.

I glare at Josh who is lying calmly on his stomach in the top bunk with his arm dangling over. "Why is your arm hanging down?"

"I want it to," he says.

"Well, don't." I turn to leave.

"Mommy, I still can't sleep," Michael whines.

"Close your eyes. It helps."

Back to the bedroom. By now the candles are flickering low, and Snoopy has landed on the floor. I toss my robe somewhere and crawl beneath the covers. Forget glamour. And boy does this negligee itch. Good grief. How did the pioneers manage to have so many kids when they all slept together in one room?

"Mommy, I'm sick."

I roll out of bed, find my robe, and turn to see Michael standing in the doorway again. Wordlessly, I take him into the bathroom.

"Let's get you a drink of water," I sigh. "Maybe that will help."

When I turn on the light, I see how flushed his cheeks are. He feels feverish, and his nose is so stuffy he can hardly breath. Instantly, I change from Kate

Capshaw to Florence Nightingale. "Poor baby," I murmur. I give him medicine and a drink of water, and once again tuck him snugly into bed. I caress his cheek and say, "Call me if you need me, baby. I'm right there in the next room."

Once more, I head back to the bedroom. I hear Rick's snores before I even reach the door; he must have come to bed and fallen asleep while I was with Michael. I blow out the candles and change into a warm flannel nightgown. In the dark, I manage to find Snoopy and drop wearily into bed.

"I guess we're just not meant to be Harrison Ford and Kate Capshaw," I whisper as I drop a kiss on Rick's shoulder.

Without waking up, Rick turns over and cuddles me close to him. I yawn, then drift to sleep with his arms around me. Eat your heart out, Ms. Capshaw.

The Park

Suzy Ryan

Finally, some sunshine! After endless El Nino-driven rains, San Diego finally experienced a beautiful Saturday. Wanting to enjoy every brilliant ray, my husband, Ken, and I took our three children for an adventure in the park at the local community college.

After lathering ourselves in sunscreen, the kids hopped on their bikes while Ken and I ran next to them. Seven-year-old Keegan sped off first as his five-year-old sister, Lauren, followed closely behind. Their younger brother, four-year-old Trent, tentatively tried his new big-boy bike, but refused to lag too far behind his siblings.

After we enjoyed a family game of baseball and soccer at the park, the hot afternoon sun left us parched for water and starved for food.

We found a picnic table and devoured our hefty lunch. Then the kids quickly jumped on their bikes as Ken and I gathered the remaining food. Running to catch them, we dissolved into a trance-like state as we witnessed the scene before us.

Keegan, our strong-willed son, raced past his brother and sister as if finishing the Tour De France. Just the day before, when I had worked in his first-grade class, I had collected my things to leave him in extended care, while I picked up Lauren and Trent from their preschool. He came to me with tears in his eyes, "Mom, can I go with you? I know you have some errands to do, but I really want some special time with you."

When did he grow into such a sensitive, thoughtful young man?

Lauren, our middle child, seemed to modify her personality to suit any situation. Even though she couldn't catch Keegan, she pedaled with fierce determination in pursuit of him.

Earlier, during lunch, she shared the last piece of cake evenly between her brothers and dad. Always willing to go the extra mile, she did not bat an eye as she served the coveted slice of dessert. *When did she develop into such a generous, compassionate young woman?*

Trent, our life-of-the-party child, refused to remain a baby. He relished the freedom of riding his new bike and not having to sit in the dreaded jogger. Although he realized that he didn't have a chance to catch his older siblings, he obstinately refused to be left behind. He rode until he said, "My legs burn." This is the boy who crawled into my lap at lunch, put his hands on my cheek, and gave me the softest smooch. "Now, you don't move your lips, Mom. I am going to kiss you." Which he did ever so tenderly, and then bounced down and finished his sandwich. *When did he grow into such an affectionate, charming young man?*

As Ken and I beheld the beauty of our children, they each seemed to be traveling on their own road of life and moving away from our control. They never looked back. We suddenly realized that this parenting process will fade quickly into the sunset. We must soak up each beam of joy this experience holds because we will soon journey to the park by ourselves to bask in the sunshine and sweet memories of today.

8
Love That Inspires

Love comforteth like sunshine after rain.
William Shakespeare

Bus Stop Roses

Linda Evans Shepherd

Jason sat on the crowded bus staring out the window. At twenty-three, he felt like the cares of the world rested on his shoulders. He worked hard at his construction job and put in long hours of manual labor. Yet his paycheck never seemed to stretch far enough, especially now that his wife, Clare, was pregnant. As he watched her ever-expanding belly, he worried. *Will I be a good provider? Will I be a good father? And what about Clare?*

He sighed. *I never buy her flowers like I used to.* It seemed his paycheck didn't allow for luxuries like that any more. He remembered her smile the first time he had given her roses. They had been walking hand in hand along a crowded street. The sunshine glowed in her blonde hair as her laughter tilted the world into a wonderland. It was Valentine's Day, and on impulse, he had paid a street vendor twenty dollars for a dozen long-stemmed beauties. He smiled as he remembered the look she had in her violet eyes when he gallantly presented them to her. Her soft smile had melted his heart.

How he longed to see her smile like that again.

Jason sighed deeply. *If only I could show her how much I appreciate her,* he thought wearily. *And here it is Valentine's Day, and I'm coming home empty-handed.*

The bus squealed to a stop, and the doors clanged open to admit an aging man dressed neatly in a faded brown suit. His kind blue eyes peered out from behind the thick lenses of his glasses, and his white hair clung above his ears, leaving the top of his head almost bare. The old man shuffled down the aisle of the bus before pointing to the empty seat beside Jason.

"Sir, is this seat taken?"

Jason shook his head. "No, go ahead."

The old man settled himself in his seat, clutching a beautiful bouquet of red roses wrapped in white tissue. Jason could smell their scent as the old man carefully held the wrapped stems.

"Are those for your wife?" Jason asked.

The old man nodded. "I've given her a dozen red roses every Valentine's day since she stole my heart over fifty years ago."

Jason smiled. "My wife loves roses too."

"How long have you been married?" the old gentleman asked.

"Almost a year." Jason surprised himself by blurting, "and we have a little one on the way."

"I hope you're doing something special for her today," the old man said with a knowing chuckle.

Jason looked down at his work-roughed hands. "I'd like to, but . . ."

The two men fell into silence as the bus groaned through city streets until it lurched to a halt under a tree-lined bus stop.

The older gentleman rose from his seat. "Here's my stop." As he stepped into the aisle, he turned back and thrust the roses at Jason. "These are for you, son. My wife would want your wife to have them."

Before Jason could protest, the old man stepped into the warmth of the afternoon.

As the bus pulled away, Jason watched as the gentleman slowly walked toward a green meadow glowing bright in the sunshine. But his vision blurred when the old man stopped at its black wrought-iron gate and pushed it open. The gate's dark, silhouetted words announced the depths of the old gentleman's generosity. They read, "Oak View Cemetery."

Leaning into Love

Jane A. Rubietta

Our morning didn't get off to a good start. In fact, it had been a hard week for our marriage—too little time together and too much to do. It added up to a chasm between Rich and me, and I stomped off in a huff to chaperone my daughter's field trip. On the way I fumed over my husband's faults, then sighed, trying to focus on the upcoming day with our daughter Ruthie.

The children's science museum was a hands-on facility. Ruthie and her classmates left their shadows on the wall, stood inside enormous soap bubbles, and experimented with magnets. One low table held sketches of various architectural structures surrounded by toy blocks. Would-be architects were invited to try their hand at a building style.

One of the suggested structures was an arch. Taped above the table were Leonardo da Vinci's words: "An arch consists of two weaknesses, which leaning against one another make a strength."

Suddenly the morning's angry words echoed in my mind—my angry words. I got the message as clearly as if God had whispered it in my ear: I brought weaknesses to my marriage. I contributed to our busyness, our opposing schedules, and the emotional distance. But together Rich and I could combine these foibles into strength.

When Ruthie and I got home, I put my arms around my husband and quoted da Vinci. We made a nice arch.

◆ ◆ ◆

A Wife's Greatest Gift

Marilynn Carlson Webber

Nate suffered a devastating blow when he lost his job. His boss had spoken curtly, "Your services are no longer needed." Nate left the building a broken man filled with despair. By the time he reached home, he was in a deep depression. When he entered his house, he blurted out to his wife Sophia, "I lost my job. I am a complete, utter failure." A tense silence followed. Then a smile crept across Sophia's face. "What great news!" she responded. "Now you can write the book you have always wanted to write."

"But I have no job and no prospect of a job," he objected completely without hope. "If I struggle to be an author, then what will we live on? Where will the money come from?"

Sophia took her husband by the hand and led him to the kitchen. Opening a drawer, she took out a box that was full of cash. "Where on earth did you get this?" Nate gasped. "To whom does it belong?"

"It's ours!" Sophia replied. "I always knew that one day you would become a great writer if only you were given the chance. From the money you gave me for housekeeping every week, I have saved as much as I could so you would have your chance. Now there is enough to last us one whole year."

What a surprise! What encouragement! What a wife! Nathaniel Hawthorne *did* write that year, and the novel he wrote became a literary masterpiece. The book is *The Scarlet Letter*.

Bernice

William R. Nesbitt Jr., M.D.

It was no secret, I was looking for a wife, not any wife, but the one God had picked out for me. God did not seem to be in a hurry, but I was. I was thirty-two years old and still in the navy serving as a doctor. Frequent changes in duty stations brought me into contact with many pretty, nice, and talented girls, but the spark was not there yet. I must admit that I was getting a little anxious.

Following World War II, I was sent on assignment to the School of Military Government at Stanford University. When I arrived in Palo Alto, I made plans to spend my first Sunday night in Berkeley at the Calvin Club (the college-age youth group at First Presbyterian Church).

I put on my dress blues with the two gold stripes on the sleeve to make an impression in case I met someone interesting. The traffic was heavy, and I was late arriving at the meeting. I was not prepared for the lightning bolt that hit me when I walked through the door. Leading the meeting was the girl I had been waiting for. She had on a purple knit dress that accented a gorgeous figure. Her exuberance was contagious, her smile captivating, and her leadership abilities impressive. I fell madly in love with her on the spot. I knew she had to be the girl God had picked out for me.

I made my way to the front of the room just as the benediction was ending.

"Hi, I'm Bill Nesbitt. You're to be complimented on the way you ran the meeting."

Some papers she was holding slipped from her hand, and as I stooped to help her pick them up, my dream shattered like a five-ton truck going through a plate-glass showroom window. On her left fourth finger was a diamond ring.

I stood up. "I see you're engaged. When is the big day?"

"Oh, not for awhile. My fiancée is back at Princeton. We won't get married until he graduates."

I left for Palo Alto totally devastated, but I continued to attend the Calvin Club every Sunday night, always ending up talking to Bernice.

Once, on a Calvin Club retreat to Zephyr Point at Lake Tahoe, a group of us decided to walk up the mountain. We came to a steep place, and I took Bernice's hand to help her.

At that moment something happened to my hand and to my heart. My hand wouldn't let go of hers, and my heart raced with uncontrollable joy. Engaged or not, I couldn't control the thrill of being close to her.

That was the last time I would see her for a very long time. I received orders to the island of Ponape in the South Pacific. Her responses to my letters were friendly but unromantic. Nevertheless, I cherished them as if they were torrid declarations of love.

A year later I returned to Oakland. The first Sunday night back at the Presbyterian Church, I was disappointed to learn that Bernice was in Nevada doing missions work. I asked her father, "When's the wedding?"

"In two weeks."

"When will she be back?" I asked.

"Oh, sometime before the wedding."

"Well, I hope so," I responded. "It would be hard for her to get married if she wasn't back."

He laughed and said, "Oh, she's not the one getting married; it's her twin sister's wedding."

"What about her wedding?" I asked.

"She's not planning one. She broke her engagement."

Suddenly the sun came out. The clouds of disappointment and despair that had been hovering over me dissipated as if by magic.

Bernice came home a week later. Our courtship was like a fantastic dream, and six months later we were married.

Forty years sped by, and the magic of our relationship was polished to a dazzling brilliance. She was an ideal wife and a wonderful Christian.

Bernice served the Lord with vigor and enthusiasm. In our own church she held numerous positions of leadership and service, including that of ordained elder. In addition to her church work, she raised three children and was involved in many community and professional activities. She taught school for twenty-five years and received many degrees, distinctions, and honors.

In spite of all she had done, she would frequently ask me, "Bill, what can we do to make the world a better place?"

"Darling, you have made the world a better place already," I answered, "especially for me."

Our lives continued to be a whirlwind of activity. Then, about ten years ago, Bernice's memory began to fail. A few years later her mother died of Alzheimer's disease. Bernice developed many of the same symptoms her mother had. As her mind and memory progressively deteriorated, it seemed obvious that her life of ministry was over.

It was hard for me to accept her condition. Being a physician, I had extensive diagnostic studies done.

The final diagnosis was multiple infarct dementia, possibly associated with an underlying Alzheimer's disease. I knew the evaluation was correct and that medically there was no hope of a cure or remission. The outcome was invariably fatal, and the progress would inevitably spiral downward.

Bernice deteriorated to the point where she slept only an hour or two a day. Because of her uncontrollable psychotic behavior, my strength finally gave out and I had to hospitalize her. There she was given powerful antipsychotic medication that calmed her down. After five days, however, I was so lonely for her that I went to the hospital to take her home. The psychiatrist didn't want to let her go. He believed she was too sick to be taken care of at home and needed to be institutionalized. But as a doctor who had cared for hundreds of demented patients in the hospital, I was sure I had the wisdom and strength to care for her myself— but I was wrong.

When she arrived home, she was drugged into a stupor. Her eyes were glazed, saliva dripped from her chin, her posture was stooped, and she walked with a shuffling gait.

I knew Bernice was dying.

The grief of losing her became real. In my mind she had already died. Even though her heart still beat and her breath still came, in her mind and in mine, she was gone. She no longer recognized me. Our marriage had never taken place, our children had never been born, and the fifty happy years we had spent together did not exist.

With tears streaming down my cheeks, I put my head down on the table and prayed. "Dear God, what am I going to do? I love her so much, and I want to take care of her, but I no longer have the strength."

His gentle voice spoke to my heart. "My grace is sufficient for you, for my power is made perfect in weakness" (2 Cor. 12:9 NIV).

I didn't believe it. I tried to put her in a nursing home, but I could not find a placement that met with my approval. Bernice was not only a very special person to me; she was also a very special person to God, and I knew in my heart that he wanted me to take care of her. Even though she could no longer remember who I was, she needed me in what, medically speaking, were going to be the last days of her life.

She continued to worsen. Each night I knelt beside her bed and prayed. The drugs she had been given in the hospital helped her sleep, but the side effects were unacceptable. When the medication was completely withdrawn, many of her psychotic symptoms returned.

Then a strange thing happened. The story of Jesus raising Lazarus from the dead came to mind. As I read the words, they took on new meaning. "'Lord, the one you love is sick.' When he heard this, Jesus said, 'This sickness will not end in death. No, it is for God's glory so that God's Son may be glorified through it'" (John 11:3–4 NIV).

Since then, Bernice has gotten better. She is less agitated and more cooperative. Best of all, I am no longer a stranger to her. I am the center of her life, her anchor to reality. Her love for me, which had been imprisoned by this devastating disease, has burst free in an overwhelming expression of affection.

A dozen times a day she will come up to me, put her hands on my shoulder, kiss me, and say, "You know I love you." Then with a twinkle in her eye, she will say, "I'm so happy."

Although she is still totally dependent and her ability to verbally communicate is extremely limited, my love for her defies description. Our nonverbal communication is ethereal. In the middle of the night I will feel her patting me, and when I move, she will whisper, "I love you."

For all our married life, I have loved Bernice with a passion. Since her illness, I discovered the wonderful opportunity I had been given to care for her. There is a tender compassion in knowing that she needs me. And there is a challenge in discovering what she wants when she is unable to tell me.

Even though Bernice is far from well, her improvement continues. It is a miracle that defies medical explanation. But there is an explanation. I know that love is healing. God gave me a love for her that is beyond human understanding, and that love has made a difference.

The Touch of Romance

Vickey Banks

It had been an excruciating year. Chronic back pain was getting the best of Cathy. A normally outgoing and chatty woman, she was retreating more and more into the quiet of her bedroom. Muscle relaxers and heating pads were becoming her friends. It was December, and Cathy's "Things to Do" list was lengthy. Needless to say, romance wasn't on the top of the list.

Cathy and her husband, Bill, had decided not to buy each other Christmas gifts because they had just purchased several pieces of furniture. However, Bill is a very generous man, and Cathy didn't trust him to hold to their bargain. Over and over again she asked him, "Are you sure you're not buying me anything for Christmas?"

"I'm sure," Bill always answered. But Cathy continued to ask.

One day Bill hesitated before answering Cathy's question. She knew he was up to something. Finally, he came clean.

"Well, I haven't actually bought you anything, but I am going to do something for you. I was going to surprise you, but you keep asking me if I'm giving you something!" He then pulled out a flyer and handed it to her. It was about classes being offered near their home. Cathy's brow wrinkled as she questioned why he had handed her the flyer. It was then that Bill said the single most romantic thing he had ever said to her.

"I've signed up to take some massage classes so I can learn how to help your back."

Suddenly, romance leapt to the top of Cathy's "Things to Do" list! She grabbed hold of Bill and told him he was the most wonderful man in the entire universe! Crying, she plied him with kisses. The next day she went shopping. He had spoken her love language, and she was determined to speak his! She walked right into his favorite sporting goods store. Grinning from ear to ear, she purchased the fly rod he had been drooling over for months. It was some Christmas!

Two months later was Valentine's Day. Bill had finished his massage training, and it was time to practice! Cathy walked into their bedroom and saw a lovely sight. Candlelight illuminated a professional massage table with Hershey's kisses laid on the headrest in the shape of a heart. Her back pain didn't completely vanish, but romance reappeared. It's amazing what a little romantic touch can do!

I Wept in His Arms

Linda Evans Shepherd

(. . . continued)

Covering my eyes with my hands, I tried to block the horror of the afternoon as I huddled under the emergency room hallway window. A storm raged outside the hospital as a storm raged within my heart. The more I fought, the more clearly I could see myself behind the wheel of my car.

The scene swirled through my thoughts: eighteen-month-old Laura snuggling in her carseat—the red tail lights reflecting on the damp pavement—my foot reaching for the brakes—my car lurching across the dividing line—the accelerating minivan . . .

A thunderous explosion of metal ripping through metal roared in my ears as my body flopped like a limp rag doll against my seat belt. The silence that followed chilled my heart. *Why, why wasn't my baby crying?*

I turned to the back seat, still expecting to reassure eighteen-month-old Laura's frightened, blue-gray eyes. Instead, I stared into a jagged, twisted metal hole.

Slipping out of my seat belt, I clawed my way through the wreckage. I was afraid of finding Laura's body smeared through the crumpled ruins. Instead, I found her in the middle of the freeway, still fastened in her carseat, dazed and still.

A doctor rushed passed me, slamming the heavy emergency room doors. Back to the present, I lifted my head, watching the staff's continued fight for Laura's life. "Jesus, help them!" I pleaded.

Soon I was ushered into the hospital waiting room.

When my husband Paul arrived, he was damp with rain and tears. I rushed to him and wept in his arms.

"Is . . . is she going to be OK?" he asked.

"I don't know," I choked. "She has a fractured skull."

We sat together silently and stared at the floor, our voices stolen by shock and grief.

The days that followed the car accident were critical as Laura fought for her life. Each time Laura thrashed with seizures, her nurses rushed her to X ray. We stumbled behind, blinded by grief.

Each CAT scan sent Laura back to surgery for the relief of the volcanic pressure building in her brain.

"We're sorry," the doctor finally said, "but Laura will never awaken. She's in a vegetative state."

Paul and I defied the doctor's wish to take Laura off life support. Instead, we chose to wait. As we waited, Paul often held my hand and let me verbally ramble through my fears and pain. It was his gentle love that supported me when our son Jimmy was born, just as Laura began to emerge from, *not* a vegetative state, but a coma. Our love and God's mercy had proven strong enough to pull our daughter back to the land of the living.

It was Paul's faithfulness that helped me endure the changes in our lives as we went from being a normal family with kids to a family with a newborn baby and a permanently disabled child on life support.

Perhaps these events did not signify the most romantic times of our lives, but there in the darkest crevasses of the valley of the shadow of death, Paul and I were forever bonded in love. We were there for each other, and when all hope was gone, we alone believed in the power of God's love mingled with our own. And that? That made all the difference.

(To be continued . . .)

9
Sizzling Anniversaries

Love can never more grow old,
Locks may lose their brown and gold,
Cheeks may fade and hollow grow,
But the hearts that love will know
Never winter's frost and chill,
Summer's warmth is in them still.

Eben E. Rexford—Silver Threads Among the Gold

Kodacolor Anniversary

Donna McDonnall

Since we were married near the end of November, we often celebrated our anniversary on or near Thanksgiving with our extended family.

As our eighth anniversary approached, we made plans to visit my parents. Our two preschool boys were excited to see Grandma and Grandpa on the farm. The day before we were to leave, our oldest son developed an upper respiratory infection. As he had asthma, we didn't feel it was wise to travel such a long distance away, so we planned a quiet evening at home.

After settling the boys for the night, I walked down the stairs, fighting feelings of disappointment and worry. As I turned to enter the family room, instantly my "pity party" vanished. There sat my husband in front of the crackling fireplace, surrounded by the warm glow of candlelight. He had plastered the walls with travel posters of the Tetons, which had been our honeymoon destination. A tape of our wedding was playing softly on the stereo.

"What's all this?" I asked incredulously.

He flipped open a photo album. "I thought maybe we could make a few memories and spend the evening looking over our 'kodacolor moments.'"

I was overwhelmed and delighted!

That night, picture-perfect memories were developed forever in our hearts.

Our Secret Forest

Bobbie Wilkinson

My husband's and my twenty-third anniversary was fast approaching. Things were very tight financially for our family with two kids in college, so I knew my creative instincts would be called upon to come up with a fitting gift for my husband.

May 1 is a wonderful time to celebrate an anniversary, as the grass is starting to turn green and flowers are beginning to poke their heads out of the ground. About a week before our special day, I was leisurely walking around our property when I suddenly looked at a grove of pine trees. Twenty-three years earlier, Tom and I had planted the pine trees as seedlings not long before our second daughter was born. Now the trees served as the perfect privacy screen as they were now fifty feet tall and crowded together so close that it was impossible to walk among them.

My heart smiled as I remembered the days when my three daughters were young and used to play among the growing pine trees. They even performed a few homemade productions in their "theater in the woods."

All of a sudden, I had the perfect idea for Tom's anniversary present. I would clear out part of this area and make a secret forest where Tom and I could walk under the enormous pine canopies and enjoy the welcome shade in the heat of our hot Virginia summers.

Tom conveniently went out of town on business a few days before our anniversary, and the work began.

I couldn't afford to hire anyone to help me, so I single-handedly began the task of sawing off the lower limbs of about sixty pine trees with a handsaw. I reached up as high as I could, as I wanted my six-foot-two-inch husband to be able to have lots of room above his head.

Little by little my clearing grew until I had created a magical secret forest that was all mine! I even bought a hammock to suspend between two trees, and two green, plastic Adirondack chairs to put in another little area. I couldn't believe what I had done during the course of a couple of days! Nor could I believe the gigantic piles of branches and limbs that were now in huge mounds on the ground outside of my clearing. We would have enough kindling for life!

I found in the underbrush an old, broken wheelbarrow. I cleaned it off as best I could, planted some bright red impatiens in it, and placed it at the entrance to my secret forest. Something was still missing, however. I picked a tree in the center of the clearing, and with enormous effort, I carved Tom's and my initials on the trunk. Now it was complete.

On our anniversary, I told Tom he had to come outside with me. With a puzzled look on his face, he followed me over to where the pine trees were all happily swaying in the breeze. (I think they were excited too!) I just stood by the entrance to the clearing and said, "Happy Anniversary!" Tom froze in place. He was absolutely stunned at what was in front of him. Slowly he began to walk through the enormous clearing, which had been transformed from a simple privacy screen to a magical retreat from the world! When I showed him our initials on the tree, an enormous grin stretched from one side of his face to the other.

Four years have now passed since I created our little fairyland out in the woods, and we still use it. Tom enjoys reading the Sunday paper out there. When our children are home, they love to sneak off and enjoy quality hammock time! So do I! Just knowing this beautiful area is there gives me a wonderful sense of peace. And when we're not using it, my secret forest is a quiet refuge for deer, birds, and other animals who also appreciate this magical place.

I don't know where the phrase "labor of love" came from, but I know that my secret forest was just that. I also know that if I had thousands of dollars to spend on an anniversary gift for my husband that year, nothing could have topped what I did for free with my hands, my time, and my heart.

A New Anniversary Dance

Lynda Munfrada

It had been eighteen years since my husband and I had playfully boxed as newlyweds. This year, for a fun anniversary present, I purchased two sets of toy boxing gloves, the kind that are so big they make you look like a toddler in your father's shoes. I wrapped them in a big box and excitedly waited for him to come home from work.

After a delicious, romantic dinner *without* the kids, I set the box on the table. His robust laughter filled the dining room as he took out the gloves, and his eyes twinkled as he challenged me to a match. Moments later, with gloves on and soft music playing, we faced each other.

I guess eighteen years is a long time. After my soft tap on his left arm and his soft tap to my tummy, something snapped. I giggled and punched him medium hard on his left shoulder and KA-WAM. I was flat on the floor.

He was still laughing. I was not!

"Ah, come on, honey! That didn't hurt, did it?"

"Lucky punch," I scoffed. The CD changer clicked, and the theme from the *Lion King* took on a new meaning.

I sprang to my feet and hunched down, ready to strike. I circled left. I circled right. I saw my chance and KA-WAM. I picked myself up off the floor again.

His face went pale, and his bright eyes went wide in sudden disbelief. "I . . . I . . . I didn't mean it honey, honest. Please calm down." No one was laughing now.

Bob and weave. Duck and punch. My father's words echoed in my brain as my husband and I danced around the table. Click. "I Just Can't Wait to Be King" urged me on.

I cleared my throat and lunged across the empty potato bowl.

"Um, honey, let's go upstairs and watch a movie or something, OK?" His voice quivered as I narrowed my eyes and pushed a chair against the hutch blocking his escape to the right. I raced around the table and landed a punch on his arm.

"Ha! Ha!" I bounced my eyebrows up and down and sneered. "I gotcha now!" I charged, giant gloves flailing.

I didn't think a man in his forties could possibly jump so high. In hurdler-fashion, he smoothly glided over the high back of the chair and ducked just in time so as not to hit his head on the swirling fan blades above the light fixture. Not thinking, I started to scramble across the table.

"Come back here, you coward!" I yelled, my knees resting in the strawberry Jell-O. Click. "Hakuna Matata" floated through the air as he disappeared through the open doorway.

I burst into laughter as I surveyed my predicament. *Lord, help me fix this one!* My laughter turned to tears as my husband sheepishly peeked around the corner. "Are you OK?"

"I'm so sorry," I sobbed and rested my chin on his chest in shame. "I've ruined our anniversary."

"No, you haven't," he gently soothed as he helped me off the table. He cuddled me in a protective "clinch," our giant gloves awkwardly encircling each other. "It was fun . . . for a minute." I'm sure I felt him smile as he said it, but he forgave me so I let it slip. Click. We stood there as "Can You Feel the Love Tonight" echoed the emotion of the moment.

Sometimes a well-planned moment goes awry. God grants us the grace to get over it and not spoil the whole evening. We survived another anniversary and are looking forward to many more. My husband said that next year he's getting us paint guns. I think I'd better take up jogging.

10
Love and Laughter

A good laugh is sunshine in a house.
Thackeray

Blind Date

Linda Evans Shepherd

(continued . . .)

Paul and I love to grab lunch while the kids are at school.

Recently, he called me up and invited me to Applebees, our favorite hangout.

"I'll be there in fifteen minutes!" I said, grabbing my black purse. I jumped into my blue Taurus and headed for the restaurant. I was looking forward to my visit with Paul over my favorite Oriental salad.

The restaurant was located in the mall parking lot, across the way from a jungle of high-tech office buildings. In fact, I often sat in the restaurant and watched Paul pad his tennis-shoed feet through the snowy field and across the railroad track to join me.

As I pushed open the giant oak and glass door, I squinted as my eyes tried to adjust to the dim light. I followed the hostess as she seated me at a table that faced the window. As the minutes ticked by, I stared into the bright snow, hoping for a sign of Paul. Except for a couple of bunnies, the field was empty. After a long while, I felt color start to rise to my cheeks. I pulled my cellular phone out of my purse and punched in his office number. No answer. *Somebody must have grabbed him for an impromptu meeting as he was leaving,* I thought, trying to bolster my patience.

Twenty more minutes passed, and now I was worried. I had sent the waiter away, and now I had no food, no husband, and I was losing faith. *What could have happened?*

Across the restaurant, I noticed a couple I barely knew from church. They stared at me strangely and whispered to one another. *They must realize that Paul stood me up,* I thought, embarrassed.

Finally, I left my seat and did a quick tour of the restaurant, making sure I had not missed my husband hiding in the crowd. No luck. I sat back down and waited. As twenty more minutes ticked by, I drummed my fingers on the table. *Paul must have headed for Chelsea's; that's where we eat when we don't meet here!*

Being that I still had no food, I decided to check out my hunch. I threw some money on the table to cover my iced tea and walked out. It was good to feel the icy air cool my hot cheeks. My car roared to life as I quickly drove to the other restaurant. Once inside, I was dismayed to discover there was no Paul. Defeated, I drove home, tired and hungry. When I arrived, I called Paul's office once more.

This time he picked up the phone.

"Where were you?" I challenged.

"At the restaurant, waiting for you."

"But I was at the restaurant," I said.

"Really? Where were you sitting?" Paul asked.

"I was at one of the round tables on the lower floor on the west side of the room."

"But that's where *I* was sitting!" Paul exclaimed. He paused, then chuckled. "The hostess must have placed us back-to-back!"

"Didn't you see me come in?" I asked.

"No, I left my glasses at work," Paul confided. "I couldn't see a thing."

"But I walked around looking for you," I said.

"That must have been when I was in the rest-room."

I told him, "No wonder that couple from church gave me such a weird look. They probably thought we were having a fight and wouldn't sit at the same table."

We roared with laughter.

We may have been sitting back-to-back, but our hearts were still in the right place. They belonged to each other.

Husband for Sale

Carol Kent

It happened again. Gene and I were in the car running errands, and I felt he was too close to the car in front of us. As the other automobile slowed down unexpectedly, I shrieked, "WATCH OUT!" Gene slammed on the brakes, and we were jolted forward.

As usual, he had plenty of room to stop, and we could have avoided this jerky reaction if I had kept my mouth shut. He was angry with me for being a back-seat driver—again. I told him I screamed because I honestly thought we were in danger, and I believed my warning might save our lives. He was unconvinced. He pulled the car to the side of the road, looked in my direction, and said, "Do you want to drive?"

Now I was hurt. I wasn't trying to tell him how to drive. My scream had been involuntary. I did not plan to make him feel like an inadequate driver. Tears blocked my vision as I withdrew into my silent martyr role. (I feel so much more spiritual when I'm not speaking.) We drove home in the thick silence of anger, hurt, and misunderstanding.

As we mutely walked into the house, our conflict was still unresolved. I left Gene in the kitchen and walked into the next room. Opening my mail, I found this anonymous letter on my desk:

Dear Friend,
This letter was started by a woman like yourself in the hopes of bringing relief to other tired and discontented

women. Unlike most chain letters, this one does not cost anything.

Just bundle up your husband and send him to the woman whose name appears at the top of the list. Then add your name to the bottom of the list and send a copy of this letter to five of your friends who are equally tired and discontented. When your name comes to the top of the list, you will receive 3,325 men . . . and some of them are bound to be better than the one you gave up!

DO NOT BREAK THIS CHAIN! One woman did, and she received her own jerk back! At this writing, a friend of mine had already received 184 men. They buried her yesterday, for it took four undertakers thirty-six hours to get the smile off her face.

We're counting on you,
A Satisfied Woman

By the time I reached the middle of the letter, I was grinning. As I finished it, I was doubled up in uproarious laughter. My confused husband walked into the room wondering what had transformed his wounded wife. Looking up, my eyes met his. "I'm sorry," I said softly. "I overreacted."

"Me too," he responded as he slipped an arm around my waist. His lips brushed the side of my face as he whispered in my ear, "Now, what's so funny?" His curiosity was killing him. And I couldn't keep a secret that was this hilarious.

"Listen to this," I said. I read the letter aloud, and both of us fell on the floor laughing until tears ran down our faces.

What Women Want on Valentine's Day

Connie Bertelsen Young

(Dennis, darling, if you happen to read this . . . I truly don't mean to embarrass you, honey, but I'm going to have to use you as an example. You see, there still seems to be some question in the minds of some men, particularly the long-term relationship types, that is, married ones, about a certain subject, and I hope to clarify it once and for all. Thanks, dear.)

I'll try to make it clear. Frankly, most men don't know what to give the love of their lives on that special day, February 14. If you are one of those men, pay attention. I'll tell you what women want.

First of all, there's no excuse for forgetting Valentine's Day. One year Dennis forgot. Becoming aware of his error, he scrambled through his personal belongings for a gift. Finding his coin collection, he withdrew a valuable silver dollar and handed it to me with these words: "Just as my coin collection is incomplete without this dollar, so is my life incomplete without you." I was speechless.

Of course women want a valentine, one with a simple message like, *"You are the most beautiful woman in the world,"* is OK; or, *"I'd rather die than live without you,"* is fine. A woman wants her man to care enough to send the very best. Last year Dennis hastily stuck a post-it note on my pillow that said he was glad he married me.

Take your time picking a gift, and remember that long-stemmed red roses will do more for your love life than you can imagine. Don't just stop at the store at the last minute on your way home from work. I still have the cheap plastic flower Dennis bought at the quick stop several years ago. He told me it wouldn't die like real flowers; like our love, it would last forever.

If you're going to buy her clothing, it should be red or black, and sexy. And if you don't want to make V-day a D-day, you better know her size. I was depressed for weeks after receiving a pair of yellow shorts two sizes too large. (Admittedly, I still have a red outfit from another time that's two sizes too small.)

Women hope for one of those gorgeous heart-shaped boxes with shiny ribbons and frills and luscious chocolates on the inside. I've never received a heart-shaped box, but once Dennis surprised me with a Snicker's candy bar. It is my favorite.

Take your woman out on Valentine's Day. If you can't afford to pay a violinist for romantic music, at least play her favorite CD. I can't say Dennis doesn't give me music. He sings in the shower every night. And as for "takeout," would you believe he gave me take-out pizza one Valentine's Day?

Curiously, single men seem more informed about what women want than the attached ones. At least that's what it looks like. Single women are the ones who show off expensive jewelry, perfume, lace, and bouquets of balloons. The rest of us want that neat stuff too, but that's not all women want.

The truth is, what women *really* want can't be held in our hands. What women want is priceless, but it's yours to give. As schmaltzy as it may seem, it's actually very simple. A WOMAN WANTS YOUR LOVE. Yeah, that's it.

Yes, indeed, my husband is a good example. A silver dollar, a cheap plastic flower, a post-it note, a candy bar, and hearing him happily singing in the shower show me his love . . . just fine.

True Love Is Blind(folded)

Liz Curtis Higgs

My plan was simple: This year I'd abduct my husband, Bill, for Valentine's Day! To pull off such a daring stunt, I knew I needed accomplices, but our offspring, ages five and seven, couldn't be trusted with any inside information. So, confiding only in two friends—one to cover the office and one to handle the baby-sitting—I began plotting our Valentine getaway.

Dinner had to come first, somewhere near home to throw Bill off track. Since he is, to put it mildly, a tightwad, we'd skip candlelight and cloth napkins in favor of a neighborhood spot with great chicken pot pie. Then, by way of a circuitous route, we'd wind our way to a charming bed and breakfast for a night of sublime passion. I could hardly wait!

Friday morning dawned sunny and perfect. When Bill took off with the kids for school and work, I took off for errands: the car wash, the bank, the hairdresser, the works.

Sitting in the carpool line that afternoon, I decided it was safe to let my kids in on the fun. When they jumped in the car, I said, "Mama has something special planned for Daddy tonight." As we headed home, I described the hours ahead, leaving out the unnecessary details.

"Why can't we go?" my daughter whined, prompting her older brother to offer, "Yeah, we could take our sleeping bags and stay in the same room with you guys!"

Oh, brother.

Once in the house, I headed for the tub. No time for the bubble bath I'd hoped for; this was the spray-and-wash special, complete with six squirts of perfume.

By a quarter to seven, I was ready. I watched the driveway with one eye and the clock with the other. Where was that baby-sitter? She simply had to get there before Bill did, or the kidnapping would lose its most vital element: surprise.

When she arrived just seconds before zero hour, I practically dragged her through the front door, stammered my last-minute instructions, grabbed our suitcases, and headed for the van. No sooner had I started the engine and popped a Vivaldi cassette in the tape player than Bill pulled in the driveway.

The look of confusion on his face turned to concern, even panic, as I marched toward him, yanked open his door, and said with a straight face, "This way, please, and no questions." I opened the passenger door of our van. "Get in!"

I knotted a bright yellow silk scarf around his bewildered eyes, put on his seat belt, then shut the car door.

"Done a lot of this kidnapping business, have you?" Bill asked grinning, when I got behind the wheel. "Where do you intend to take me?"

"You'll see," I replied, then drove the short distance to our dinner destination and pulled into a parking space.

"Can I take off the blindfold now?" Bill asked, lifting a corner to peek out the bottom.

"Of course," I said, as he slid off the yellow scarf and tossed it on the dash.

"Great!" Bill said when he saw the restaurant selection. "My favorite chicken pot pie. We should be home by nine and still get a good night's sleep."

I looked at him sideways. A good night's sleep was not what I had in mind, but I let it pass. "Come on," I said. "Our pot pie awaits!"

Unfortunately, every serving of the house favorite had already been gobbled up by early birds, so we had to settle for beef stew and a table jammed between the swinging kitchen door and a harried couple with three kids under five.

"Feels just like home," Bill said with a smile, but I found it increasingly hard to be cheerful. After a less-than-satisfying slice of pie, we made our way toward the door.

Bill looked at his watch. "Mind if we stop at the hardware store?" he asked, climbing in the car. "I just need a ratchet wrench."

"Sure, why not," I said, sighing noisily. While he looked for his wrench, I looked at my watch. Our hostess at the B & B expected us by nine; if we left right away, we'd only be half an hour late.

"Store's closing, time to go!" I said as brightly as I could, tearing Bill away from his fascination with lug nuts. Once in the car again, I grabbed the blindfold and extended it towards him. "Put it on, please."

"To drive home?" he asked, beginning to look pale around the ears.

"We're not going home," I announced, starting the car.

"Liz, what are you talking about?" he asked, his voice sounding oddly strained.

"No more questions!" I repeated, turning toward the expressway. "Just sit back and enjoy the ride."

"Can you just tell me what time we'll get home?" he pleaded, sounding a bit desperate. I looked toward his scarf-swathed face. "I don't know, honey. About noon, I guess."

"Noon?!" he almost shouted, yanking off the blindfold. "That's way too late!"

"Too late for what?" I asked him, beginning to get concerned myself. Now he clammed up.

"Well, uh . . . we need to be . . . up early," he said slowly.

"On a Saturday?" I said, almost veering off the road.

"Never mind, it'll all work out," he said, turning toward the window to end the discussion. We drove in silence for nearly ten miles; then he asked me softly, "How far from home are we going to be, exactly?"

"Exactly sixty miles," I answered. A slight groan escaped his lips before he fell silent again.

"Bill, if you don't want to do this, we can turn around and go home. We'll lose the money, of course, but if you . . ."

"NO! Not a problem, don't lose the money!" he said with sudden enthusiasm. "Wherever we're going, it'll be terrific."

His mysterious behavior confused me, but I decided to make the best of what was left of our evening. We chatted until the moment we pulled up to the B & B. "We're here!" I said triumphantly.

"Doesn't it look romantic?"

"Sure," he said climbing out, but I could tell he wasn't sure at all.

Once inside the Victorian home, we headed up a narrow staircase to our room, which turned out to be cozy and inviting.

"How about I take a quick shower?" Bill suggested as I unpacked. "Maybe this night will be salvaged after all," I thought, hanging our clothes up in the antique wardrobe.

Bill's "quick shower" turned into the usual thirty-minute hot water extravaganza. At last, he dripped his way back into our room, warm and wet and freshly shaved. "Nice," I said, brushing his cheek and flashing my most beguiling smile. "I'll be right back."

Five minutes later, when I tiptoed into our room after brushing my teeth and adding yet another squirt of perfume, I found Bill snoring soundly in our king-sized bed.

"Ah, well, mornings are nice too," I thought as I sighed loudly and climbed under the quilt. But sleep didn't come easily for me. Tossing from side to side, punching at my flimsy feather pillow, I finally joined my husband in "Snoreland" well past midnight.

But not for long.

The next thing I knew, Bill was leaning over me, fully dressed, shaking me insistently. "Liz! Wake up!" he whispered, then with more volume, "LIZ! We gotta get going or we'll be late!"

"Huh?" I asked, squinting at him through the darkness. "Late for what?"

"For your Valentine surprise, that's what!" he said, obviously exasperated.

I sat up and looked at the clock. "Bill, it's five-thirty in the morning!"

"Right, which means if we hustle, we'll make it back home by seven." He yanked my covers off and handed me my clothes. "I'm ready when you are."

"But we haven't even had breakfast yet—and that's included with the room," I said, sliding my feet to the floor.

His frugal heart skipped a beat. "Oh. Sorry about that," he said, then brightened. "We'll drive through McDonald's on the way!"

"On the way to where?" I asked, pulling a comb through my hair and buttoning my sweater.

"You'll see!" he said, guiding me down the dim staircase and out the door.

"I'll drive this time, and you wear the blindfold."

Now I knew how ridiculous Bill must have felt, riding along in a cloth-wrapped shadow. "We didn't even have time for breakfast," I moaned again. "Or anything else."

The hour-long drive passed quietly. We got ham-and-egg biscuits at the drive-thru, and the coffee perked me up by the time Bill made a final turn and switched off the ignition.

"We're just in time," he said, touching my blindfold. "Ready?"

"I guess so," I said. The scarf fell from my eyes, and a gasp rose to my lips. Directly in front of our mini-van was a huge, rainbow-colored hot air balloon, fully inflated, straining at its tethers. "Oh my word; is this for us?" I asked.

"Just for us," he assured me, reaching across to open my door and giving me a gentle nudge in that direction. I almost fell out of the van as we made our way over to the gondola of the waiting balloon.

"Thought you forgot!" the pilot said, reaching down to help me in. Bill scrambled in behind me, and the crew stepped forward to help with the launch.

Like Dorothy, Toto, and the Wizard himself, we began pulling away from the ground, slowly at first, then accelerating as the pilot tugged on the gas jets and the air in the balloon filled with a fresh burst of heat.

The view below was extraordinary, the sensation of joy in my chest even more so. Fighting tears, I turned to Bill. "Why didn't you tell me?" I whispered.

"Look who's talking!" he whispered back, rolling his eyes. "I had this planned and paid for weeks ago."

"Probably about the time I made our reservation at the B & B," I thought wryly. "Do they only fly at the crack of dawn?" I asked him, waving with happy abandon at the cows below.

"Oh, no, they have afternoon flights too," Bill said, then added, "but, it's a little cheaper in the morning."

I should have known.

11
Working Romantics

Success is sweet,
but its secret is sweat.

Unknown

Cheering to the Finish Line

Bill Farrel

It's not always easy being teammates. Pam and I had a several-month-long disagreement over her desire to spread her wings. She wanted to return to school and begin work on her writing career. We had a plan and she wanted to jump ahead of schedule. And I didn't like it!

We still had children who were at home full-time. Pam was a great mom. She was also a great wife, lover, and friend. Her desire to chase her goals put pressure on me to help with domestic duties beyond what I thought should be expected of me. Pam's dreams were an inconvenience to my life! And as she looked outside our home for growth, I was missing her. My response was to get angry with her. I fought her for months before I came to my senses. I realized I wasn't fighting Pam; I was fighting God. God had placed this dream in Pam, and I was blocking it. Pam wasn't trying to make my life miserable—I was choosing that for myself.

I finally came to the point where I could encourage Pam in her pursuits and wanted to find a way to make up for the grief I had given her. One day I had to be on campus for a project we were working on at church. Pam would be in class on that day, and before she left for school, she said, "Think of me when you are at school today."

That's when I got an idea that was as big as the resistance I had been throwing in Pam's way.

She was in a medieval literature class that morning. The professor was leaning against the chalkboard and had just announced that romance was dead. He pointed out that it was an idealistic fallacy in the middle ages and unobtainable today. A chorus of women in the room agreed, "Yeah, all men are jerks."

In the middle of this invective on the state of men in our world, I broke into the room unannounced. I walked over to Pam's desk, which was inconveniently located in the middle of the room. I set down a dozen red roses on her desk, bent down over her left shoulder, whispered, "I love you," gave her a kiss, and left the room as quickly as I had come in.

"Is it your birthday?" the startled professor asked Pam.

"No."

"Your anniversary?"

"No."

"Then what's the reason?"

"I guess he just wanted me to know he loves me and he believes in me!"

Then many of the women in the class asked, "Does he have a brother?"

I had fought Pam in a big way as she tried to pursue her dream. I wanted her to know in just as big a way that I believed in her dream.

Put Your Calendar Where Your Love Is

Terry Paulson

I was trapped, and a part of me knew it. Yet, getting out of a trap I enjoyed was hard. After all, the world told me I was successful. My life was working, but it was working in overdrive, and I didn't know how to find an offramp.

At that time in my life, I was a successful professional speaker. At my best and worst, I was speaking two hundred times a year wherever they would have me. If there was a date available and they wanted me, I was ready and willing to help leaders and workers make change work. I was making a difference for audiences and for our family's bottom line. But something was wrong. There were no vacations, no breaks, and little time with my son and my wife.

I had been on the road for over a week. I was ready to be home. I found my car in the airport parking lot, threw in my luggage, and put my mind on autopilot— "T. P., drive home!"

My wife let me put my things away, a nice touch in retrospect. But as I walked down the stairway, she asked me to stop to talk. I recognized her tone as serious and thoughtful, so I took a seat. Gently, she said, "I've struggled with what I am going to say to you for a long time."

I could tell from the tone of her voice that I was in big trouble. She continued, "I know how much you love what you do. In fact, few people I know love what they do as much as you do. I know you make a difference to people you talk to. But I did not marry you not to see you."

Her tone was emotionless, and I knew humor was counter-indicated. But to tell the truth, her words brought home the trap I was feeling. True, I loved what I was doing, but I was burning myself out.

I eventually did use humor, a gift that on more than one occasion has helped keep our twenty-two-year marriage so satisfying. I said with a smile, "At least you're saying you want me here. After all, you could be saying, 'You're making so much money, why don't you just stay out there and send that money home!'"

Thank goodness she laughed. Thank goodness we both wanted to find a way out, a way to make it work.

The conversation continued with occasional tears meandered through a valley of pain and hope. We realized again that love must be worked, not assumed. Love requires time together. It was time to put my love where my calendar was.

After all, we had made time when we were dating. Unfortunately, after the marriage, the dating stopped. We'd been there, done that!

That night we decided to date again and to purchase season tickets to the theater.

We made a point of scheduling our vacations and treating them like business commitments. If someone wanted me to speak during a scheduled vacation, I would say, "I already have a commitment." The person did not need to know what my commitment was, and I did not need to defend or argue my choice to find balance.

I must confess that at times I have traded for a different vacation date, but my wife always has the right of refusal; and sometimes I give up my tickets to take care of unplanned, urgent needs of customers or friends, but it doesn't happen often.

Our struggle for balance reminds me of a conversation I had with a man from India on a flight from New York to Los Angeles. We talked about our wives and lessons learned. He admitted that he was at times puzzled by Americans and their search for the perfect love. He had been amused by how hard we work to find someone we love, and then we assume that love will last once the right person is found. Like many in India, his marriage had been arranged. He knew that there was no love to begin with but worked hard to make love come alive. He confided that he felt sorry for Americans who assumed that love would just last. For to him, love always took work. The work of love should show in your calendar. It now does in mine, and it makes all the difference.

For Richer for Poorer

Martha McNatt

"Plug in the potpourri pot," said my husband on the phone. "I'm bringing a prospect for the house in an hour." He believed strongly in the power of a pleasant aroma upon a real estate prospect.

"But Honey, we agreed we would keep this one," I protested. We had been through this eight times before. My husband, Alex, is a master at matching people with houses, and eight families are living happily in homes that once were ours.

I have enjoyed the new houses. I don't even mind the packing and unpacking. I have hauled my mother's one hundred-year-old rosebush to eight locations, and it blooms happily wherever it is planted. For each move, I transfer plants and bulbs, but I leave something of myself in each location. I can identify my plants as I drive by all the houses we have lived in.

"Our house is exactly right for these people," Alex said excitedly. "And I have already spotted another house for us. It has a bigger kitchen, more light, and an office all your own; and it's already landscaped."

I had to admit I felt a twinge of excitement, but I was weary of moving. Our friends were beginning to make remarks like, "When are you going to move? You have already been there two years."

Nobody knew that the financial gain we had made on every sale had enabled us to invest in a vacation house that became our romantic getaway.

Each house we purchased had special features, which we could enhance by investing our physical labor. Alex is an excellent painter. I am good at combining colors and decorative tricks. Together we can transform a bland house into a custom-decorated look with a few gallons of paint, some wallpaper, a few yards of fabric, and hours of labor.

When we pledged our marriage vows, we promised to support each other in all things. We have not failed. Our love has deepened, and our friendship has sustained us as we have worked together on this avocation while maintaining separate careers. I can feel the excitement I hear in his voice when he talks about a new house. I can visualize the house he describes to me. I feel a rush of adventure and a twinge of nostalgia as I look around the house I have loved, if only for a short period.

I picked up the overnight clutter and plugged in the potpourri pot.

Best Friends

Lenae Bulthuis and Diane Zuidema

As best friends, we love many of the same things—writing, reading, and eating chocolate. We also love the same type of men. Our husbands are both hard-working farmers. They're sensible men who are too busy in the here-and-now to waste time on frivolous dreams and impractical visions. That's fine, except for the fact that what we, their wives, thrive on are frivolous dreams and impractical visions. So if we want to share an exciting dream, we have to telephone each other. "When our book makes the best-seller list, I'm going to tell Oprah . . . ."

One afternoon we complained that our husbands didn't seem as confident about the many best-sellers we were sure to someday write. So we decided to enroll in a writing class at a local university. Halfway through the class, we were elated (and somewhat shocked) to have three homework assignments purchased by a regional magazine. Still, we couldn't convince our husbands that our long-awaited call from the Oprah show was just over the horizon!

A couple of weeks later, the four of us slid into a booth at a local restaurant for a quiet dinner. As if on cue, our husbands headed to the bathroom and didn't emerge for ten minutes. When they returned, the waitress took our orders. When she left our booth, one of our strong, silent John-Wayne-type husbands cleared his throat and pulled a piece of paper from the inside pocket of his leather jacket.

Looking rather sheepish, he unfolded the paper and glanced across the table at the other husband who was just breaking into a sweat. "OK. We have a presentation tonight," he announced awkwardly. "We have two awards—two achievement awards." He looked up at us with a nervous smile. "Would you please hold your applause."

We giggled.

He continued, "These two awards go to two women who are involved in church and school activities and they work outside the home. They also have children and, not to mention, demanding husbands.

"Even with all that, they went to school and excelled. They wrote articles that are going to be published." He cleared his throat. "So, with no further ado, I am honored to give these two awards to Lenae and Diane for first articles published. Would you please come forward for the award."

We gasped in surprise when, from beneath their jackets, the men pulled engraved plaques, bearing our names, the date, and the beautiful words: "First articles published."

While we had been complaining about "those men who just don't understand us," they had been planning this private awards ceremony to validate our impractical visions and join in our frivolous dreams.

We flushed with the excitement. Perhaps we were married to men with far-reaching vision after all! We'll be sure to mention that when Oprah calls!

12
Romantic Getaways

Wherever you are, I am there also.

Beethoven

The Affair

Pam Farrel

It was a surprise. Over dinner one night, in casual conversation as we were coordinating our schedules—as usual because we always have to hunt for moments to steal away and be together—my husband said he was going to have to go to a convention for work. My heart sank. *Away again,* I thought. Just thinking about it made me miss him. I felt like I was always having to share him. He noticed the change in my countenance and muttered something like, "It's only a few days," and stroked my hair reassuringly. I nodded knowingly and said, "It's just that we get so little time alone."

The next morning, after I knew he'd left the house for work and started his day's appointments, I called his office. I can't remember just what I said to get the information, but I acquired the name of the hotel where he would be staying for the convention. Then I made a call and begged a friend to come stay with the kids.

The day was a flurry. I packed the picnic basket with candles, chocolate, two glasses, and a bottle of sparkling drink with a big bow. I remember it well because the bow covered the very small thing I packed to wear later that night. I grabbed a portable stereo and bought a new Kenny G cassette. He loves jazz, I wistfully recalled. I threw in my makeup bag along with a toothbrush.

On the way out of town, I stopped at the mall to buy a new outfit. A night like this needs a new outfit.

Something he'll remember. Something that will stop him in his tracks and make him smile at me with that look—that look that makes me melt. *It has to be soft,* I thought. *And a good color—and it has to make me feel—well, great!* After several attempts, I slipped a long azul sweater over tight black leggings, and I knew I'd found it! I longed for his touch.

Back in the car, I listened to love songs on the radio. The station seemed to play all the songs we'd ever danced to or sang to each other in whispered tones under soft lights. I found that I was leaning more and more forward in my seat, as if my heart was being drawn to him. The lights from the oncoming cars on the freeway seemed to dance and flicker. It was probably just a normal commute to most, but not to me. Tonight was going to be special—a secret rendezvous, a liaison. My heart raced as the odometer clicked down the miles. As I turned on the exit ramp, I felt my heart pounding, my desire for him was becoming so strong I thought I could hear my own heartbeat—just like I had heard his so often after we'd been together intimately. I loved to lay quietly in his arms and rest my head on his chest. I breathed deeply and felt as if I could smell that deliciously familiar fragrance of his aftershave.

I parked the car discreetly behind a nearby business. His business partners and associates were also at this conference, and I couldn't take any chances at being seen or having my car recognized. I looked at my watch and sighed in relief. I had timed it just right. They would all still be at the banquet, so I'd have time to sneak into his room undetected.

I must have seemed a little flustered when I asked for the room number and the key because the desk clerk mumbled, "Oh, I'm sorry, ma'am, the register only has one registered for that room." A little panicked, I managed to pull myself together, and I answered as confidently as I could, "Oh, I'm his wife, and he really wasn't sure if I'd be able to get off work to come." He nodded his head like he believed me and handed me the key.

I quickly walked across the parking lot, my arms full of the packings of a woman in love. I glanced at my watch again. *I'll have to hurry to get everything set up. I want the atmosphere just right when he steps into the room,* I thought.

And it was just right. Soft flickering candlelight danced across the ceiling to the mellow sound of the smooth saxophone as he stepped into the room. He saw me standing there in the shadows. He stared at me in stunned amazement. I knew at that moment that I had recaptured his heart. As I ran to him, he wrapped his arms around me, twirled me around, and whispered, "Wow! What a surprise. I'm so glad you've come."

Then we kissed and danced and did all the things I had dreamed we'd do. Finally, we fell asleep in each other's arms. My long blond hair fell scattered across his chest, and it all felt so good—so right—and I could hear the beat of his heart as I lay there.

The quiet beeping of my watch alarm was an unwelcome sound the next morning. I knew I had to go, but I didn't want to. Why can't these moments last forever? I quietly slipped into my clothes and gathered up the staples of romance I had brought with me. I ran my fingers through his hair, and we kissed. He thanked me again for coming, and he smiled that smile as I closed the door behind me. As I drove out of the parking lot, the sun was peeking up from its slumber, and a hint of sunlight spilled across the steering wheel. It caught the corner of one of the facets of my diamond ring—the ring my husband had given me fifteen years before. I smiled. *No guilt,* I thought, *just an affair to remember—an affair with my beloved husband.*

Unexpected Blessing

Ellen Bergh

Most people chart a course for a driving vacation with detailed maps, planned rest stops, and orderly travel. We are not those people. We'd been married fifteen years before we embarked on a vacation on the road. We planned to just go with the flow.

The itinerary looked like a no-brainer. Los Angeles to Yosemite to Portland, Oregon, and return. What could go wrong? At Yosemite we rafted in the green waters of the Merced and savored the forest glade. The discord developed during the repack of the Datsun truck for the next leg of the trip.

I'm a morning person, the rabbit type raring to be on the road at first light. My husband, the turtle type, slowly stowed the camping equipment with such precision you'd have thought he expected border inspection by the "Perfection Patrol." I stood by mentally drumming my fingers. Finally, we left Yosemite at 10:30, which put us on Interstate 5 through central California during the 100-degree day. As a hot wind blew through the tiny truck, I came to a slow boil, replaying in my mind how this all could have been avoided, if only he'd listened to me. I told him we needed to get going earlier. The eternal day ended after a two-hour tie-up in traffic. We wearily pulled into Stockton in the early evening and peeled ourselves off the hot seats. I flounced into the motel room, sulking over the ordeal we'd been through. While my family frolicked in the pool, I lay on the bed projecting what horrors lay ahead tomorrow if we got another slow start.

Later that evening, noticing my glum mood, my husband asked, "What would it take to make you happy?"

"I'd be happy if we don't dawdle along like today. We need to be on the road before dawn so we can avoid this heat. Then I'd feel we'd be making some progress."

My victory seemed hollow at 5:00 A.M. the next morning when we trooped out to the truck. Our lanky daughter refused to ride up front with the feuding folks, preferring to perch on top of the camping gear. We pulled onto Interstate 5. The euphoria of yesterday in Yosemite a memory, we rode along in strained silence. Not more than ten miles out of Stockton, in the predawn, sat a car stranded beside the freeway. I cringed. My husband traces his lineage back to the good Samaritan. Surely he wouldn't think of stopping. Didn't he know we needed to press on to be out of the hot central valley? But as we passed the car, we saw a man and woman and three little girls in frilly party dresses shivering in the back seat.

My husband looked over at me, and I reluctantly nodded. He pulled over onto the shoulder and backed up to the disabled vehicle.

While the men set to work with his tools, my daughter and I dispensed old sweatshirts and donuts and fruit juice to the lady and the kids. She told us they'd been to a family reunion in Stockton and got a late start home. Their car died, and all night long, they watched people whiz by without stopping. The girls cried themselves to sleep. While our daughter stayed with the girls, the woman and I settled in our truck. We exchanged stories of how both of us had read the riot act to our men the night before. We shook our heads and hoped to do better.

Their car fixed, we caravaned to their turnoff in Sacramento. As we waved good-bye, my husband met my gaze. We burst out laughing. Both of us knew whose timetable we were really on. I shoved my map under the seat and scooted closer to him. In helping someone else, God had healed my road rage and restored our joy in the journey.

I Think We're Alone Now
(Are You Still in the Mood?)

Nancy Kennedy

I had a rendezvous with love. Earlier, I'd scribbled a note for Barry to meet me in the lobby of the poshest motel in town that fit our budget (the one the guy on the radio guaranteed would leave the light on for us). Then, tossing a new black satin nightie into an overnight bag, I kissed the girls good-bye and sped off.

Barry and I needed this time away together. For some reason, we hadn't been connecting lately. Barry had been working long hours and often came home exhausted. He barely had enough energy to gobble down dinner before he hit the shower and crawled into bed. On the nights he did come home early, he'd often find me in my office working at the computer or at the dining room table pouring over lists of song titles.

On those rare nights when both of us were awake and lucid and interested in, well, you know, the presence of our offspring (who get their second wind at 10:00 P.M. and think it's child abuse to suggest they go to bed the same time we do) quickly and effectively doused any and all sparks that may have ignited.

Fortunately, there's always Auxiliary Plan B. I learned it from my own parents. Once my siblings and I were teenagers and could stay by ourselves, our folks would pack an overnight bag, kiss us all good-bye, and spend the night away from home. Of course, back then I didn't fully understand why they had to leave home, but now I know.

After arriving at the motel and finding our room, I changed into my nightie, tuned in some mood music on the radio, and waited for Barry to walk through the door.

First, I posed myself on the bed, then I switched over to the chair, then back to the bed. Finally, I remembered the suggestion Marabel Morgan made in her book *The Total Woman*. Surprise your husband by pouncing on him as he enters the room.

I climbed up on top of the dresser and crouched in wait.

And I waited . . .

And I waited . . .

By the time Barry finally opened the door, I'd discovered that the part of my body that's supposed to be able to crouch and pounce had stopped working back in my thirties. My sexy, surprising "Tada!" instead came out as a pathetic, "Help! Get me down from here!"

Once he'd helped me down, Barry turned on the TV and flopped onto the bed. "Man, I'm beat," he groaned.

Not a promising sign.

I collapsed my stiff, aching body next to him as he lay there with his eyes closed. "Just let me take a ten minute nap; then I'll take a shower, we'll go get something to eat, then if you want, we'll (yawn) . . ."

We stayed in that position until morning.

So much for a wild and passionate night. Luckily, my husband and I aren't the type to give up easily. We tried again the following week; only this time I skipped changing into the nightie and the crouching and pouncing part. I was still trying to decide my modus operandi when Barry burst through the door.

"How about a kiss?" he asked and pulled me close. I blinked at him in surprise. (It amazed me how my romantic mood can go from red hot to "you've got to be kidding" in a matter of seconds).

"I'm sorry, but you have to woo me first," I informed him.

Now it was Barry's turn to blink. "Woo? What 'woo'? We've been doing this for twenty years!"

"How about some music?" I asked, then turned on the clock radio and went into the bathroom to draw a bath. Barry mumbled something unintelligible over the roar of the faucet and the air conditioner as I eased myself into the cool water. *Yes,* I thought, *this is definitely going to be a night to remember.*

Once I'd stepped out of the tub, smoothed my skin with lotion, and slipped on my robe, I slunk out of the bathroom, ready for ministry. Except—Barry was gone. No note, no clue, just gone. (Note: Nothing kills a romantic mood faster than one party disappearing.)

Where could he be? I wondered. My thoughts ran the gamut: He stepped out for ice; he found someone else; he'd been abducted by pod people. After fifteen minutes went by, I finally panicked, but not before I mentally dissected him. *I can't believe it! He's always doing this to me, like it's macho not to let me know where he is!* By the time I was through, I didn't care if the pod people had turned him into one of them.

By then it was dark, and I was barefoot and dressed in my bathrobe. I walked around the building a few times—no sign of him anywhere. The oddest part was his truck was in the parking lot next to my car.

I went back to our room and opened the door. Again, no Barry. By this time I was utterly exasperated and terrified out of my mind (not to mention ticked to the hilt). I wasn't, however, about to go back out and look for him again. Instead, I went out on the balcony to watch and wait.

While I was on the balcony, it started to rain, and I reached for the door handle to go back inside. That's when I found myself stranded; the door to the balcony was locked from the inside.

So, with Barry out only God knew where, I crouched under a chair to shelter myself from the storm.

Talk about obstacles to intimacy. This scenario beats insomniac kids any day. I began to cry, "Barry!" I called between sobs. "Barry, where are you?" I pleaded with God to bring him back safely and confessed every known sin on my conscience. Suddenly, wooing didn't seem all that important. I just wanted Barry back safely.

Finally, as quickly as the rain started, it stopped, and once it did, I heard the motel room door open.

"Barry! I'm out here!" I called. By the time he let me in, I was a sopping, shivering mess.

I looked dreadful, with my hair wet and plastered to my head and my eye makeup smeared all over my cheeks. My pink robe, once a fluffy soft velour, had turned heavy and muddy. Not quite the look of a "total woman" out to seduce her husband.

We held each other tight. "Where were you?" I cried.

"I told you I was going out for Chinese food."

"I didn't hear it. You should've told me louder."

"You should've listened louder."

Our passion rose, and the mood turned. . . .

Sometime in the middle of the night, I awoke and went back out on the balcony. I gazed up at the stars and smiled.

The Best of Times, the Worst of Times

Marita Littauer

It was almost noon when we finally pulled out of the dock into the gray fog that enveloped Newport Harbor. It was early May, and the fog should have lifted by now, but this was El Nino, and all the weather patterns were confused. Due to our late start, we motored out of the harbor with my husband, Chuck, at the wheel and me sitting on the bowsprit to watch for oncoming boats that might appear through the haze.

Once out of the harbor, we were anxious to sail to Catalina Island to celebrate our wedding anniversary. However, there was still no sun peeking out of the muck surrounding us and not a breath of wind. We motored past Bell Buoy Number 1 and gawked at the ever-present seals sleeping all over each other despite the incessant ringing on the bell just above their heads.

We moved on in the general direction of Catalina Island. My hair blew slightly. *Hah! Was that wind?* Thrilled, we abandoned our course and sailed for the wind.

An hour later Chuck began to show the first signs of seasickness. The slow bobbing through the ocean had taken its toll. He managed to stagger below and collapse on one of the sleeping areas. I urged him to come topside. "I don't want to be too far from the bathroom," he moaned.

By now the wind had picked up, and the sailing was getting really good.

This was why I like to sail. The sun was shining, the wind was blowing, and no other boats were in sight. The bow crashed through the oncoming waves and the wind was coming from the perfect direction. I was in heaven.

But as time went on, the wind increased, the waves mounted, and I was beginning to feel like a tiny speck in a vast and angry ocean. I looked down below. Chuck was resting comfortably, rocking back and forth with each swell, while I was wrestling with the wind and the boat. The sun was getting low on the horizon, and the air was getting brisk. I zipped up my red down parka, pulled up the fur-trimmed hood and donned my thick red winter gloves. The port side of the boat was nearly touching the water, and I fought to keep myself upright. The waves, now white-capped and six feet high, crashed against the bow as I pressed the boat through them. Repeatedly, sea spray hit me in the face, causing me to gasp in surprise.

As I held on for my life, part of me said, *This is some of the best sailing I have ever had. I'm loving this!* Then another wave crashed over the bow, sloshing water all over the topside and hitting me in the face. That's when the other part of me said, *I am going to die!* My next thought was, *too bad Chuck's going to miss it.* Then the famous Charles Dickens' line, "It was the best of times. It was the worst of times," began to play in my mind as I volleyed between *this is the best sailing I have ever had,* and *I am going to die!*

For hours I loved the wind but feared the waves. Finally Avalon Harbor came into view. The sun had slipped over the horizon, and the lights of Avalon twinkled on. I was exhausted and exhilarated at the same time.

Chuck was still resting quietly below. I hated to wake him, but I really thought it was time to drop the sails and begin motoring toward the harbor. Weighing my options, I headed the boat into the wind, locked down the wheel, and began the climb to the bow. I was battling the jib as the wind threatened to rip it from my hands. I was so focused on what I was doing that I did not see Chuck emerge until I heard the engine roar to life. He pointed us back into the wind, and I felt a huge rush of relief. I finished dropping the jib and then dropped the main.

Safely back in the cockpit, I clung to Chuck. I asked, "What made you get up?"

He said, "When I was laying there, I saw your feet go by the window. I realized what you must be trying to do, and I knew you couldn't easily do it alone."

He was feeling better and stayed at the helm all the way into the harbor, but I collapsed into a heap.

Looking back, I realize how much this day paralleled our lives. Even though I am a capable sailor, I do not want to sail alone. Neither do I want to go through life without Chuck.

In seventeen years of marriage, we have had good times and bad times—even bad years. But we remember the good times and know that we love and need each other. When I am weak, he is strong. When he is down, I can lift him up. Just like that day of sailing—it is better together.

Without Words

Dianne E. Butts

As the sun sank in the western sky, the shadows of the mountains grew, casting a chilly shade across the valley below. I tugged my leather coat tighter around me.

The quiet motor of our Honda Goldwing paused as Hal downshifted and we leaned into a corner. Around the bend, the road straightened again as we zigzagged our way above lakes and timber toward the mountain's summit.

Just then, Hal reached back, placed a gloved hand on my knee, then jumped slightly—as if startled to find me there.

"I'm still here," I said, leaning forward to put my chin on his shoulder.

"Just checking," he said, turning slightly—our helmets clicking as they bumped.

Hal and I have toured the nation's highways, back roads, and national parks together by motorcycle for more than twenty years. Even while on the motorcycle, we can still carry on a conversation. But after so many hours of riding, the conversations cease. Still, we communicate—he pats my leg; I rub his shoulders; he nods his head to the beat blaring through the radio into our headsets.

Whether we're rockin' and rollin' or riding in silence, I treasure these moments when we find ways to say, "I'm glad you're here," "I enjoy your company," or "I love you" without words.

On a Mountaintop in Norway

Charlotte Adelsperger

In 1961 I absorbed the exciting adventure of being in Norway, where I attended the University of Oslo International Summer School. I was fresh out of college and learning all about Norwegian culture. I looked forward to sharing all I was learning with my fourth graders in the states. Best of all were the field trips with students from many different countries.

One weekend my travel friend, Karin Lindahl, and I took a long train trip from Oslo to Bergen. We delighted in the marvelous views of mountains, farmlands, and the contrast of passing through numerous tunnels. For a moment I closed my eyes and thought about being back in St. Louis where I would face life as a first-year teacher and single person.

Karin and I loved the historic coastal town of Bergen with its bustling open-air markets. But I shall never forget our second day there. We rode the funicular, or mountain cable car, to the top of Mount Fløyen, one of the seven mountains surrounding the city. We were captivated by the awesome view of houses, the harbor, and fjords. While Karin went into a shop, I ambled down a path to a quiet spot overlooking Bergen. Those moments have always remained with me.

That night I wrote in my diary about my time alone on that mountain path on July 21, 1961: "Today on Fløyen, I came to a lovely place where I saw rich moss among the trees. I spent time in silent prayer. As I stood there, I visualized the painting of Christ I had seen the day before in Johanneskirke, an old church in Bergen. It showed Jesus, head bowed, praying alone on a mountain with the light of dawn breaking over his shoulders. I opened my whole self to God and asked him to guide my personal life as both a single and a teacher. As I prayed I turned over to God my deepest desire—to find the husband right for me.

"May I always remember the serenity and power on the mountain overlooking Bergen," I wrote. "Today was a day of dedication. After my walk when I neared the cafe to meet Karin, the Norwegian orchestra, coincidentally, played 'Wonderful One,' a sweetheart song I know from college!"

After I returned to the states, I dated several prospective mates, but none seemed to be the one. Three years later, when I was teaching in the Kansas City suburbs, I met Bob Adelsperger, who had recently returned to the States from air force service on Okinawa.

I landed Bob as my bridge partner through a church group. Now there was a man with qualities! We dated, fell in love, and were married in June 1965. Of course, I told Bob all about my prayer for a husband on that mountain in Norway. Our years together proved he was my "wonderful one." Even our two children, Karen and John, have heard the Bergen story—a number of times.

When Bob and I planned a trip to Europe in 1998, I insisted we include Norway. We traveled the same scenic train route to Bergen. As we took the funicular to the top of Mount Fløyen on a sunny June afternoon, I could feel my heart speeding up.

At the summit, Bob and I strolled hand in hand and wide-eyed as we looked down on colorful Bergen. "You were right. It's beautiful!" Bob said.

"Come this way," I urged, tugging his hand. "I'm taking you to the spot where I prayed. It may take a few minutes to find it—considering that was thirty-seven years ago!" But there it was, lovely view and all! Thick moss still covered the ground. Bob and I were all smiles as a Norwegian snapped our picture. We hugged.

"I thank God for you," I whispered. Then we kissed, and the camera clicked again.

13
Moments That Sparkle

Ah! Memories of sweet summer eves,
Of moonlit wave and willowy way,
Of stars and flowers, and dewy leaves,
And smiles and tones more dear than they!

Whittier-Memories

The Night Charley Pride Sang to Us

Don Haines

Trying to maintain a happy marriage in these hectic times can test the mettle of even the strongest love. When both husband and wife work, the stress of running a household and raising children can make life sometimes seem like an endless treadmill, with little time for each other. In order to maintain their sanity, a couple must have something they can turn to that will take their mind off their problems.

It needn't be much. For some, a walk in the woods on a warm autumn day might be their therapy.

For others, sitting on the back porch on a moonlit night will rid them of their cares. For Sheila and I, it's a song.

I first heard Charley Pride sing on my car radio in 1967. His smooth baritone voice came from his lungs and larynx, but the song came from his heart. I became an instant fan, and it would be a Charley Pride song that would see Sheila and I through some of our most difficult times.

During the early years of our marriage, whenever Sheila would get down, I'd try to comfort her by saying that someday things would be different. We wouldn't have to work so hard. Our children would be on their own. We'd have more money, and I'd spend all of my time repaying her for all of her sacrifices. I'd usually end these little pep talks by giving her a hug and saying, "I promise you baby . . . one of these days."

One of These Days

I'll spend more time with you,
I'll do more things for you,
To show you how much I love you
One of these days.

One of these days, one of these days,
When our children can share us,
When our duties can spare us,
When our problems fade away,
One of these days.

One of these days, one of these days,
When my job don't demand me,
When my work leaves some time free,
When our fortune is made,
One of these days,

One of these days, one of these days,
Till then please believe me,
And don't ever leave me.
Believe me when I say,
One of these days,
One of these days.

It was the lead song on side two of Charley Pride's fifth album. It was much less than a hit for Charley, but it was a monster hit for Sheila and me. It spoke to our hearts during many a trying time and would be "our song" for the next thirty years.

There were times during those years when Sheila had a hard time coping with the heartfelt lyrics of "One of These Days." It was during those times I'd hold her and say, "just wait honey, that's us, that's our song, it will come true."

By the summer of 1998, I'd finally delivered on my promise. Sheila and I sat on the deck of our empty nest, two retired people, still in good health and ready to enjoy the rest of our lives together. She was reading the paper when she mentioned that Charley Pride would be doing a concert at the Great Frederick Fair on September 22, 1998.

"Charley hasn't been around here for a while." I said. "I'm going to get tickets."

It was then the idea hit me. I found Charley's address in Dallas, Texas, via the Internet. I told him the story of how "One of These Days" had become our song and how Sheila and I had used it for inspiration through the years. I explained how our "One of These Days" had finally gotten here, and I could finally give Sheila the attention she deserved, that we'd be in the audience on September 22, and how much it would mean to me if he could sing "One of These Days" as a surprise for my wife.

When we went to the concert that night, I didn't know whether Charley had gotten my letter, or whether he'd do the song. Entertainers get many requests. To meet them all would be impossible.

Charley was seventy minutes into a ninety-minute show, and my hopes were slowly fading. Then, he finished a song, turned and beckoned to his steel guitar player, who brought him a sheet of paper. The great Charley Pride started talking. "When I got back from England, I had a letter from this fellow who wanted me to do a song as a surprise for his wife." He then went on to tell our story, and ended with, "Are you out there, Don?"

I grabbed Sheila by the shoulders, and we both stood up. "We're here Charley! Thank you!" Then with the spotlight on us, I kissed my wife in front of thousands of people. It seemed appropriate at the time. Charley thought so, too, and said so. Just before he sang, he explained that he hadn't done "One of These Days" since he recorded it in the 1960s, so he would need to see the words on paper. Our song was really ours. It was apparent that it hadn't touched anyone else like it touched us. With the spot still on us, in front of thousands of people, Charley Pride sang our song, and he sang it to us. The crowd cheered heartily when the song ended and Charley shouted out, "Were you surprised, Sheila?"

With tears in her eyes, Sheila replied. "Yes Charley! Thank you!"

When we were driving home that night, I glanced over at Sheila and thought back to the young girl who'd taken a chance on me so many years ago. We'd had some bad times and some good times, but none better than the night Charley Pride sang to us.

Lovebirds

Georgia E. Burkett

Christmas gifts at our house during the Great Depression were always scarce. Mother usually gave us practical gifts such as clothing, books, and toilet articles. But Daddy never failed to come up with some kind of surprise.

The afternoon of Christmas Eve, 1938, Daddy was very late coming home from work. Mother waited anxiously, for she had not yet been able to do any Christmas shopping because she was waiting for his paycheck.

Besides, the house rent was due. I was a teenager then, old enough to share her concern. So Mother and I prayed, asking God to bring Daddy home in time for her to go shopping.

Finally, just as the sun was setting in the wintry sky, Daddy marched up our sidewalk, carrying a huge package colorfully wrapped in Christmas paper. My sister and brothers yelled, "Here he is, Mother, and he's got a great big bundle of something."

Mother, understandably upset, demanded as Daddy came into the house, "Where have you been, Sam? You know I've got to go shopping!"

"Calm down, Mother," Daddy replied. "You'll never guess what I brought you for Christmas. But you'd better open it right away."

"Humph," Mother grunted, refusing to even look at her gift.

We kids weren't angry though, and we weren't about to wait for Mother to investigate. We all pulled string and paper off that package until with one big gasp, we cried, "Mother! Look what Daddy brought you!"

With a chuckle, Daddy put his arms around Mother and said, "It's a pair of lovebirds, Mom, in a cage. Just like you and me."

No way on earth could Mother resist laughing. It was ridiculous. Daddy had saved enough money for her to buy us a few Christmas gifts, but the rent money he spent for a pair of beautiful green parakeets.

Even though Christmas gifts for the rest of us were very scarce that year, we kids didn't care. Mother and Daddy loved each other enough to forgive and forget petty annoyances, and we knew that was a gift more priceless than gold.

Of course, the rent got paid anyway, and the memory of that day will live in my heart forever.

Lilacs

Maggie Mae Sharp

Lady National Cowboy Poet of 1996

I want to plant lilacs with a man that I love
together, to dig in the soil . . .
For somehow it seems
that more lilacs will grow
with love, and with four hands to toil.

I want to plant lilacs with a man that I love
'round a cottage built by our own sweat and tears
For although it may fall, or burn to the ground
love and lilacs, will last through the years.

For there isn't a road you can take in this life
whether Eastern or Western, you go;
When you won't pass an abandoned old homestead
where the chimneys stand alone in a row.

And the wood has been burned,
and the bricks toppled down—
sometimes even the trees are all withered away;
But the lilacs remain, and they bloom every year—
and they multiply more—with each passing day.

So, if I were to plant lilacs with a man that I love
together, to dig in the soil . . .
Still somehow it seems
that more lilacs will grow
with love, and with four hands to toil.

First-Time Father-to-Be

Steve Standerfer

When Carolyn called me in Sweden to tell me the doctor said the baby would come prematurely, I flew home immediately. But now, she was two weeks overdue. It seemed the baby would never come.

Tensions mounted as the sweltering August heat beat down relentlessly in our hot desert community of Antelope Valley. It was no place for a pregnant lady, or her first-time father-to-be husband!

I tried in vain to make my wife comfortable. I loved her so much, and I longed to do something for her—anything. But our swamp cooler did little to ease her misery, and our tight budget couldn't stretch to afford an air conditioner.

"Will this baby ever come?" my wife groaned.

"Of course it will, Love," I comforted. "You're doing just great."

"No I'm not, I'm dying," she moaned. "I've gained forty pounds, and this heat is killing me! I wish I could jump in a pool and cool off."

Then it hit me. *That's it! Get her to a pool, but where? Did I know anyone with a pool?* That didn't matter, I would find a way. I was a desperate man.

I began making telephone calls all over the city, hoping for a solution.

Finally I got a "Yes!" Wasting no time, I carefully helped my wife into the car, and we headed to the highway. After a short drive, we pulled in alongside a well-manicured lawn and fragrant rose bushes.

Checking in at the office, the man recognized me as the one who had just called. He handed me a pen. "Sign here."

One five-dollar bill later, we were registered as guests to use the motel's swimming pool for the afternoon.

I watched my wife waddle into that pool and finally find refreshment, not to mention weightlessness. It was such a relief—to both of us.

Looking back over the years, and several children later, I have to laugh at myself as that frustrated, frightened first-time father-to-be. I've changed a lot since then—except for one important detail: I still love my wife, and there's little I wouldn't do to show it.

Time Out!

Bonnie Compton Hanson

I've no time for Time—
There's never enough,
What with eating and sleeping
And breathing and stuff.

I'm behind from the dawn
To the setting of sun.
Almost finished? Forget it;
I've scarcely begun!

In fact, the one time
That I've time for Time
Is when the day's over,
All's quiet, and I'm

Standing here with my love
In my arms. What a thrill!
Oh, please, Time, stand still!
(I will if you will!)

Romance in the Rush

Sue Cameron

After fifteen years of marriage, I just discovered my husband Craig has this . . . habit. He reminds me of love. On Tuesday nights at 6:30, with Bible Study in our home at 7:00, I am frantically throwing dishes into the dishwasher and frantically issuing orders, "Josh, Sar, Aime, Eric, finish your homework and go upstairs!"

"But Mom," says Eric, "I'm only in kindergarten. I don't have homework."

"Then help Josh with his," I scream.

"But Mom," says Josh, "I'm in seventh grade. I don't think he can help me much." I scowl at them both.

That's when Craig strolls in the kitchen—cool, calm, and collected. I thrust the coffeepot into his hands, "Make the coffee," I demand, but he doesn't. He puts the pot down. He takes me into his arms and tells me I am beautiful. He says, "I like the look of a hurried women."

Normally I sigh and roll my eyes. But not tonight. Tonight, after fifteen years of being loved when I'm a raging maniac, a wonderful truth sinks in.

Although he's never said it in words, Craig is reminding me of an eternal truth. Love is the greatest of all. Love will remain. Dirty dishes won't remain. Hectic moments won't remain. The self-implored pressure of this hour won't remain. Love will. Love is the important thing. Let's not miss this moment. Let's enjoy the love.

So, in an uncommon response, instead of yelling at my husband to "Help me do all this stuff," I kiss him back. It is nice. Much better, I think, than yelling.

The coffee gets made. The dishes get washed. And I am reminded that this moment is worth enjoying because love will always remain.

Savoring Simple Pleasures

Karen O'Connor

One late afternoon, after a long day of raking pine needles and pulling weeds at our weekend cabin in the mountains, I hobbled into the house, exhausted. My husband, Charles, stayed behind to put away the gardening tools. As I stepped into the shower, my mind wandered to all the things left to do before our little hideaway was just the way I wanted it: wallpaper for the bathroom; new carpet for the living room and bedroom; and, pretty curtains for the windows. Of course, it would also be nice to buy a new sofa bed and a matching chair and some kitchen dishes and pictures for the walls and . . . A hard rap on the bathroom window pulled me out of my fantasy. I peeked out, and there stood Charles smiling at me, his face smudged, his eyes bright.

"What's up?" I called over the pelting water.

"Not much," he answered. "I miss you, that's all. The sun's almost down," he added gently, pointing toward the mountains, "and I want you here beside me as the day ends."

A little shiver ran down my spine. Here was a gesture so simple and a gift so lovely that it took my breath away and brought me down to where I ought to be. What did it matter, in that moment, that we didn't have everything in place? We had each other. We had this day. We had the simple pleasure of watching, arm in arm, the golden sun slip behind the hills.

Summer Storm Passing

Debbie Brockett

Leaves rustled down upon the grass as a blustery wind nearly folded our globe willow in half. Holding hands, my husband Ben and I were somewhat sheltered from the elements by the deep porch. Off to the south, flashes of lightning followed by rumbling thunder rolled across the slate sky. Fascinated, we waited for the summer storm to pass.

I shivered, more from thinking about recent family troubles than the chill in the air, and Ben slipped his arm around my shoulders.

"You all right?"

I nodded and snuggled closer to his side. "Love you."

"Love you too, Hon."

Rain began to spatter at our feet, and icy moisture blew in our faces.

Tucking his feet under the swing, Ben said, "Not going to be a quick one this time."

"They never are, dear." I wasn't talking about nature's storms. Within moments the storm hit with uncharacteristic fury. I shook my head when Ben suggested we go inside. Somehow the storm seemed to draw my hidden anger and frustration to the surface and carried them away in a drenching swirl. As quickly as it came, it diminished. The rain dripped like diamonds off the willow's leaves, and a patch of blue emerged on the horizon. My spirit felt as cleansed as the fresh air.

I leaned my head against Ben's shoulder. No matter what storm needed weathering, he was always by my side.

"Seems the storm's passed."

"They always do, Dear. Love you."

"Love you too, Hon."

14
Romancing the Heart

When I give I give myself.
Walt Whitman—Song of Myself

The Bracelet Promise

Carmen Leal-Pock

The glitter of green stones drew me to the solitary display case. The light bounced off the silver and glass. Amidst the jumble of holiday shoppers, I made my way to the corner area reserved for fine jewelry and gazed upon the bracelet, noticing the unique handiwork. The beaten silver, fashioned in such a way as to resemble diamond chips, was delightful. Seeing dozens of dark green emeralds, I knew this was a one-of-a-kind treasure.

As I stared in wonder at the intricate piece, I remembered a promise my husband had made. David had bought me a lovely gift four years before on our honeymoon. He had selected an emerald green Austrian crystal and seed pearl bracelet in honor of my May birthstone. As he fastened it on my wrist, he lovingly said, "I promise you that soon I will buy you real emeralds. Just wait." Though I loved the honeymoon gift, deep down I looked forward to David's promise.

Until that time, however, I still delighted in wearing the delicate creation. I wore it frequently, each time remembering the island boutique. Whenever David saw the bracelet, he remembered his promise and would reassure me that the time was coming soon when he would keep it.

It became our habit over the years to look in every jewelry store window as if searching for the Holy Grail. We wandered in and out of countless shops, becoming discouraged when we realized the cost of the promise was well beyond our means. I soon wavered in my belief that I would ever own what David desired to give me. However, David never lost faith.

Now we were in the mall, during the last week before Christmas, to buy gifts for our children. Finances were tight; we had agreed there would be no exchange of gifts between us. We had just completed one of the most stressful years possible. With David's diagnosis of Huntington's Disease, our lives had forever changed. This terminal, neurological disorder had pitched us into a panic, not to mention near bankruptcy.

I looked up from the case into David's eyes and saw love shining even brighter than the stones. I could tell in his mind that nothing short of this bracelet would satisfy his honeymoon promise, but I knew there was no way we could possibly afford it. I tried to tell him, but the words died on my lips. He'd had so many disappointments this year that I didn't have the heart to tell him the answer was no.

Thinking fast, I came up with a reason to decline what I knew was an offer I could not accept. I have large wrists, and normally bracelets don't fit. As the store clerk reverently lifted the object out of the case, I knew it would be too small.

The silver and green made a colorful contrast against my brown skin. I silently acknowledged how much I wanted this bracelet, while hoping it would not fit. As the clerk reached around my wrist and closed the intricate clasp, my heart both plummeted and leapt. It fit! It was perfect; yet I knew there was no way we could afford it. The unpaid bills, with more looming in the future, had placed a vise around our checkbook.

I glanced at my best friend and saw his shining smile burst forth. This man, who had never hurt anyone, was now the victim of one of the cruelest diseases known to man. His was a sentence with only one verdict. Death. Untimely, slow, and cruel death. My eyes brimmed with tears as I realized we would not live out our dream of growing old together. To David, this was not just one more bauble in an already overcrowded jewelry box. Rather, this was his love displayed on my arm for all the world to see. To David, a promise made was a promise kept.

I sadly realized that he might not have many more months or years to keep his promise. Suddenly it became the most important covenant ever made. Somehow I had to juggle the bills to let him have the honor of keeping his promise.

"Do you like it?" he whispered, with hope in his voice and a love in his eyes that I am sure few women have ever had the privilege of experiencing. It was clear that David cherished me. All he ever wanted, from the day we met, was to please me.

"Yes, honey, I love it." I answered. "It's exactly what I want."

The clerk reached for my arm to remove the bracelet. I could not believe this little object had worked its way into my heart so quickly.

"How much is it?" I finally asked. Slowly the man turned over the little white tag. Two-hundred fifty dollars, it read. Surely it was a mistake! I had seen enough to know that price was only a fraction of its worth.

The man began to extol the virtues of the item, pointing out the 180 emeralds in a handmade Brazilian setting. But even though $250 was an incredible price, it might as well have been $2,500, for all we could stretch our meager budget.

Without thinking, I asked, "Would you take $225, tax included?" I surprised myself at that question because shops in malls do not normally bargain.

He looked at me in surprise and answered, "That will be fine."

Before he could change his mind, I whipped out my credit card, all the while watching as David beamed with pride. The man quickly handled the transaction, and we were on our way. Every few steps we would stop and look at the bracelet. Before we reached the car, David said, "When I get sicker and eventually die, you need to look at each emerald. Each one will remind you of something special we've done—a trip we took, a movie we saw, or a moment we shared. This will be your memory bracelet." I began to cry. David's concern was not his own failing health but for how I would handle life without him.

As we worked our way home in the bumper-to-bumper traffic during rush hour in Honolulu, I wondered just how we could pay for the bracelet. Oddly enough, I never really panicked; I was just somehow curious how it would all work out. We talked as we traveled and every so often looked at the miracle of the promise kept.

On the way into the house, I grabbed the mail and began to open it as we walked inside. Amidst the usual bills were two cards. I opened the first, which was from a church where I had sung several times that year.

It was a thank-you note for my music ministry along with a gift. I was speechless. I was looking at a check for two hundred dollars! I reached for the second card and slit it open. Out fell two bills; a twenty and a five. The card was simply signed, "A friend in Christ."

I looked up at David, and we both began to laugh. I remembered how I had felt the need to ask the clerk if he would take $225, tax included. Even as we were in the mall, the payment for David's promise was in the mailbox. God had already taken care of every detail, including the $25 plus tax.

It is just a piece of jewelry. Something I could have lived without. But the memories attached to our time together have helped to make me the woman I am today. The exquisite joy and the unspeakable grief of this relationship have grown me in ways I could never have anticipated.

The promise David spoke on our honeymoon had been fulfilled. It was only through God that we stopped at that shop on that day to find that specific bracelet. The pastor of a small church, coupled with an unknown friend, listened to God as they decided their holiday giving.

When I wear my emeralds, I pull out memories I have tucked away in my heart. Dave kept his promise.

◆ ◆ ◆

I Love Getting Flowers!

Kathy Collard Miller

"Our fourth wedding anniversary is in a few days," I mused as I sat down, more and more aware of my bulging stomach. I was pregnant with our first child, and I didn't feel very good about it myself. It was hard to consider myself as sexy or desirable. "Sometimes I wonder if Larry still looks at me the same way. If he would buy me flowers this anniversary, that would really let me know he does."

As June 20 got closer and closer, my hopes for flowers increased, even though he had seldom brought me flowers. I reasoned, "He should know how important this is to me. I'm sure he'll come through."

June 20 finally arrived. Unexpectedly, the doorbell rang. I opened the door to find a florist delivery boy holding a beautiful spray of long-stemmed red roses. It was gorgeous! My heart beat with excitement. *He does love me,* I thought. *He actually thought of it himself!*

I was eager to open the card and see the romantic words Larry had written. The card read, "Congratulations on choosing us to build your new pool. We know you'll love it."

The flowers weren't from Larry at all; they were from the pool company with whom we had contracted to build our pool the previous week!

Suddenly I started laughing. "Lord, you do have a sense of humor. You allowed these flowers to arrive on my anniversary so I wouldn't be too disappointed when Larry arrives home empty-handed. I see now how unrealistic my thinking is."

I had known Larry hated giving me flowers because he didn't like the fact that they died. I just couldn't convince him that they were valuable to me—by just receiving them—even if they did die. As the years passed, his attitude stayed the same.

Several years ago, after twenty-three years of marriage, Larry planned something that totally surprised me. We were speaking at a Valentine's Day banquet for couples, and near the end of our presentation, Larry began talking about our different opinions of flowers, which wasn't part of our planned talk. I stood there, wondering what in the world he was doing.

Then Larry pulled out from within the podium an exquisite real rose covered in 24k gold. As the audience clapped in delight, I was caught totally off guard. In my delight, I leaned over and gave him a tender kiss. That rose sits in a glass vase on my desk as a constant reminder that even old husbands can learn new tricks.

What a difference from that anniversary years ago. Because Larry has come to understand my need for romance, he has been willing to fulfill my definition of it, even though it's not the same as his. In fact, for the last three Christmases, he has presented me with a bouquet of long-stemmed roses. But there's still one aspect of flowers he doesn't understand: why I dry the roses and keep them—when they're dead!

More Precious Than Roses

Sandy Cathcart

I watched my friend's husband wrap a shining diamond bracelet around her thin wrist. The brilliant
stones filled an inch-thick circle of real sterling silver.
Tina's face lit with joy as she caught her husband's loving look.

My heart sank. It wasn't even her birthday, or
Christmas, or anything. I remembered when my own
husband used to bring me roses and special little gifts
simply for the sake of showing his affection. Now, the
lack of roses always pops up in our arguments. "You
never bring me roses anymore," I say. Then he rolls
his eyes and throws his hands in the air. Following one
argument, he brought home a potted plant. That was
the closest he ever got to granting my request for cut
flowers.

I watched Tina and Scott join in a warm embrace.
"Guess I'll be leaving," I said. "Beautiful gift, Scott."

"The perfect thing for a beautiful woman." He
didn't look at me as he answered. He was still staring
into the eyes of his enraptured wife.

I sulked on the way home, wondering if my husband would bring me flowers if I were thin and beautiful. Then I switched from being sorry for myself to
being mad. Why couldn't my husband think to do the
small things that make a woman feel special?

About halfway home, I realized the silliness of my
thoughts. My husband may not bring me flowers, but
he is forever faithful. I never have to worry about

where he is or what he is doing; he is my best friend, always willing to listen when I have a need; he provides me with a comfortable home; he is gentle and kind; he even calls from work to say that he misses me. What are roses to all of that?

On the flip side, I thought of Tina and of the many times she had called with a complaint about her wayward husband. "His drinking is getting really bad," she told me recently. "I'm happier when he's gone than when he's home."

By the time I reached the door of my own home, I greeted my husband with a long embrace. He returned my symbol of love, then looked questioningly into my eyes. "I'm so thankful you're my husband," I said, "even if you never bring me roses."

He just shook his head and muttered something about not being able to understand women. Then he asked me about my day. As we talked comfortably over cups of steaming cinnamon tea, I silently whispered a thanks to God for showing me the value of a gift more precious than diamonds or roses.

Heart-Fulls of Love

Dave Mattingly

Before we were married, I'd stop, now and then, to buy Linda some flowers. Since I didn't have a car, I'd have to carry the flowers as I walked to her apartment. A couple of times, passing motorists jeered at me. I'd only laugh. After all, anyone rude enough to yell remarks at a stranger probably did not have such a love in his life as I did.

One morning, when Linda and I had only been married a couple of weeks, I got up early. I felt such overflowing love for her, I just had to do something special.

While she slept, I made paper origami rosebuds with drinking straw stems. I put them in a plastic cup and put the cup in a place where I knew she'd see them. I also wrote a note, which read, "Since we've been married, I haven't had the money to buy you flowers, but I want to remind you how special you are to me."

After that, I cut out one hundred paper hearts. I wrote, "I Love You," on each one and decorated the entire apartment with them. The hearts were taped to the walls, doors, and furniture. But what really got to her were the ones she found in the coming weeks. They were hiding in the utensil drawer, under the last towel in the bathroom closet, stuck behind the last check in her checkbook, and hiding in a side pocket of a suitcase. They kept turning up everywhere!

She still says it's the most romantic thing I've ever done for her (though I've never stopped trying to top it).

Every time a heart turned up, it reminded her of my love.

A Special Gift

Orallee Robinson

I looked up from my mixing bowl and out the kitchen window in time to see a white-tailed deer leaping across the rich green field of sugar-beet tops. Pushing a strand of stray hair out of my face, I went back to mixing the batter for a loaf of banana nut bread I was baking. I had been promising Tom for some time now that I would make him a loaf. I glanced at the bovine shaped clock over the window when I heard a pickup pull into the drive. I wasn't expecting company.

I set my bowl on the counter and started wiping my hands on my country-blue checkered-pattern apron as I walked to the back door. Reaching the screen, I noticed the pickup was Tom's. He was home early for lunch, I guessed, so I slipped on my tennis shoes and went out to meet him. Before I reached the pickup, he opened the door and came toward me with his arms stretched out, waiting for his daily lunchtime hug. We embraced and squeezed each other tightly. Once he released me, he continued to stand where he was. I was expecting him to follow me into the house to eat. I realized he had not moved away from the pickup, and now he was smiling from ear to ear. I turned around asked him what was so funny.

I half expected him to tell me I had flour on my face or that he just loved me and that I was beautiful. Instead, he shook his head, motioning for me to come back to the pickup. "I've brought you something," he said. I was waiting for him to tell me he brought home a stray puppy or kitten, neither of which we needed.

He reached out for me to take his hand as he closed the pickup door. I complied and slipped my hand into its required position, nestled snugly within his. He led me around the back of the pickup to the passenger side. Then he opened the door and stepped back, revealing my gift. A two-day-old Holstein calf—a baby steer for me to care for and raise. I have a special fondness for livestock and wild animals, and in our eleven years together, this was the first living gift he had given me. I started to cry as I knelt down to look into the dark, shiny blue eyes of my new pet.

After all these years together, he really was listening to me when I told him what I truly wanted when we had the room.

In His Hands

Karen O'Connor

One year while my husband was establishing a new career, I took advantage of an opportunity to earn some additional money to tide us over. But the strain of keeping everything going—our home, family, church work and my usual writing and teaching—began to get to me. I was suddenly resentful of my self-appointed role as super wife. "Dear Lord," I prayed one day as I flew home from an exhausting two-week consulting job out of state, "you know my needs and the needs of my home and family. I can't do it all. Please work it out. I'm too tired to even think of a solution."

I arrived home later that day to a sparkling clean kitchen, freshly-scrubbed bathroom, and a newly-painted living room, dining room, and hallway. Every picture and painting on our walls (and we have a collection to rival any small museum!) and every dish and glass in the china cabinet had been washed, polished, and replaced. The furniture throughout the house was freshly oiled, and the carpets perfectly vacuumed. The "angel" behind all this? My husband.

"Just wanted to surprise you," he said, smiling from ear to ear. "If you can help with the earnings for awhile, it's the least I can do to help with the chores around here. Welcome home, honey!"

I glanced heavenward and whispered a humble "Thanks!"

The Three Men I Married!

Pamela F. Dowd

I have been married to three kinds of Rodneys over the past two decades. The Rodney I met right after college asked my father for my hand in marriage, but he never proposed to me. He claimed bragging rights among his fraternity brothers. He didn't have to bend a knee to a woman. It never occurred to him that his boast offended me. When I brought it to his attention after the newlywed sweetness dampened, he said, "You married me, didn't you?" As a young attorney, he made an unarguable point. I looked at the traditional solitaire diamond ring and remembered June 10, 1978, the day of our wedding. Though he hadn't officially asked me to marry him, he'd given me his solemn vows that day—vows we both intended to keep.

The week before our tenth anniversary, June 10, 1988, Rodney and I fought long distance. I was 150 miles away at a work-related conference. Each phone conversation left me in frustrated tears. I arrived home five days later in a foul mood with a sour disposition. I knew it was the end of a difficult relationship, and as much as I didn't want to leave the marriage, I convinced myself that he wanted out.

When I arrived home, I only wanted to see our three children. Rodney was the last person I wanted to spend time with, but he was the only person waiting for me. He suggested a walk downtown in the heat. The vapors rose from the sidewalk on that June day, and steam seemed to be pent up inside me as I tried to feel happy to be home. As we walked he tried to engage me in small talk. He took my hand. Sweat mingled in our palms, and I thought of all the sweat and toil that had gone into keeping both of us sane through so much fighting over the years. Our marriage felt like the dry leaves clinging to the trees under which we walked.

He said, "Sit down," and indicated the courthouse steps.

I knew what was coming, and though I didn't want it to happen, I felt unprepared to stop it. I held my breath, shut my eyes and waited for the word *divorce*.

"Would you marry me again?"

My eyes popped open as I said, "What?"

Rodney held a ring box gingerly before me. He laughed a gentle laugh and dropped down on one knee. "I said, would you marry me again?"

As he opened the box, a deep blue sapphire and diamond ring caught the sunlight and winked at me.

I let my held breath out with a rush and said, "Yes!" I'd never been more startled.

"I didn't like you being gone this week," he offered as an explanation for his incessant fights.

"That's what all that was about?"

He looked sheepish, but he nodded and grinned. "Surprised you, didn't I? You said you'd do it again, and now you can't take it back."

I smiled at him and thought to myself—and so I will do it again.

As we walked home hand in hand, the leaves didn't seem as dull; I'd finally gotten my down-on-one-knee proposal. This time though, I entered the "engagement" with less hope than I'd entered the marriage. Proposal or not, things had to change. We talked about that too.

We changed all right, and when the third Rodney came to propose, he did it with a flourish and a gentled heart.

The morning of our twentieth anniversary, he called me from work. "Let's go to the Versailles exhibit in Jackson, Mississippi, today," he said, as if it were normal to take three-hundred-mile day trips. I've learned to say "OK" over the years to my impetuous husband, so I willingly agreed.

The trip was pleasant. We talked and laughed and shared our dreams.

Before we crossed the Mississippi River, he suggested we change drivers. We stopped at a small convenience store, and while inside, he snuck out the back door to retrieve a small box from the glove compartment. When he slipped back inside, I was buying Jr. Mints to celebrate. I never knew he'd been gone.

Back on the road again, we soon approached the Mississippi River Bridge. Right in the middle of crossing, he popped a ring box open and held it at the height of the steering wheel. "Will you marry me?" he asked with a grin plastered on his gorgeous face.

The sun glinted off the diamond and emerald ring. I gazed at the green ring against the backdrop of the verdant bridge high above the water below; it's a wonder I didn't crash the car. Rodney had planned the perfect proposal for me, his incurably romantic wife. We exited on the other side and talked a security guard at the Mississippi hospitality center into capturing the moment on film. All my questions of when and how were answered with a hug and a smile. He'd been listening to my heart and taking notes for twenty years; he knew me well.

It's like I always tell young brides, "You don't often get the sensitive caring husband you long for on the day you marry him. That process takes years. You grow there together."

15
Romantic Good-byes

Good-night, good-night!
Parting is such sweet sorrow,
That I shall say good-night till it be tomorrow.

William Shakespeare, Romeo and Juliet

Blessed Preservation

Nancy Bayless

Sometimes I want to scream! It's devastating to watch the mental deterioration of my strong, . . . tall, gentle husband—my stern and splendid mate. His fine mind is off somewhere . . . frolicking through autumn leaves, I like to think. It comes home when I least expect it to amaze me with its intellect, logic, and humor that never sleep.

Sometimes I want to giggle when I see my husband slipping into bed fully clothed with his hat cocked in jaunty defiance and his wallet and car keys tucked in the side pockets of his jeans. Though he hasn't started a car in years, he keeps his keys ready to open the driver's door for me and pat me in with gallant care.

Watching him "check out" is like an amputation—a tearing away. Then he smiles. His smile takes off in his pale blue eyes, crinkles his entire face, and lands in my heart.

His smile is God's gift to me. It wraps a golden halo around my season of sadness. I am so blessed to receive the special gifts God scatters throughout my days. And I know my season of joy will come again—when my husband enfolds me with an eager hug—on a street of gold in heaven.

The Perfectly Matched Pair

Rose Hampton Newton

A smile sprang up from Jacob's happy heart and lit up his whole face. It spread all the way up to the dull glow of his bald pate. He could barely keep from licking his lips as he began to relish another chance to talk about life with the only woman he'd ever loved, Jennie, his wife. "We courted slow," Jacob said, "had to 'cause Jennie had a labor of love to her family that wasn't finished yet. She couldn't do no marriage with less than her all, and that wasn't hers to give for a lot more years. Jennie's ma was bedfast. She wasn't just sick, she was plum worn out with having a dozen kids. What with Jen being the oldest, her job was cut out for her before she would give anything but her heart and her promise to me."

Jennie chuckled. "I knew he really loved me, waiting fifteen years like that, and me being too old to have any kids for us by the time we could marry." The love he'd lavish on her during both that fifteen-year wait and their twenty-five years of marriage resonated through her words and through the smile she favored upon him as she spoke.

Jake beamed with pleasure while Jennie spoke. Smooth as silk, he countered, "Think about it, folks. I was getting some bargain. Jen has the sweetest spirit, and it just got better as we went along. Not only did she do what had to be done, she done it and had fun at the same time. And she's like that the biggest part of the time. She was a good girl; she loves the Lord.

She's always been purtier than a picture. The two of us together hasn't never missed out on one thing, friends. We've had it all just being together."

Love is something Jake and Jennie do, but it's feelings too. And this time was no different than any other time we visited them in their three-room basement apartment. That apartment was their palace because of the love they shared there.

Memories tumble out of both Jake and Jennie. Though they both can barely contain themselves waiting for the other to finish so she or he can begin to share the next one, they are always gracious with each other's space. Just as she is patient with his passion for puzzles, he is with her passion for sharing how she acquired each and every one of her knickknacks.

One day they talked about Jake's plowing up a nest of snakes as he walked behind a team of mules one afternoon. He was so scared that he literally leaped from the ground up onto the back of one of the mules. The mule was so terrified that he broke loose from the plow and carried the three of them out of striking distance of the snakes. "Had good yields that year we sharecropped for Sam and Becky," Jake said while shuddering at one memory and smiling at the other.

Memories of helping to raise and becoming, for all practical purposes, grandparents to the six children of another couple they lived with for years satisfied any yearning either of them had for being parents. Life had indeed been full for these two.

They'd never had a house of their own, but they had spent many years lovingly polishing the house of the Lord where they worshiped twice on Sunday and at mid-week prayer meeting. "Me and Jen," Sam said, "have never missed a meal or much of anything else cause we've always given his tithe back to God. He kept that old car running until I couldn't drive any-more too." Then Jen chimed in, "He feeds us good. Remember them boxes of fruit Lucy brings by twice a month? She says when she's at the store, she finds this box with our name on it and brings it to us before it spoils."

At no time did Jake mention the cancer he was dying from or the tiring doctor visits and sickening treatments. Neither did Jennie, though they both knew that his time, and theirs together, was short.

They were right. That was in early November, and by mid-December Jake had gone home to his Lord. The most he ever said, even during intense pain, was, "Take me home, Lord. Please take me home."

Jennie let him go there easily. She knew she'd join him some fine day and that he'd still be loving her just as he already had for so long. And she did just that a few months later. They found her in her bed as if she were peacefully sleeping. You can bet that neither of them has slept since. That perfectly matched pair has forever to sit at the feet of Jesus and to finish all that leftover loving from this side of eternity.

"Heaven and all this too," must surely be the lyrics to their newest, sweetest duet.

Our Love Lingers On

Randolph Ed Arrington

I see the house we built for our home
And I see the love that we knew,
And tho you are gone our love lingers on
But I just can't see me without you.

Sometimes in my life midst labor and strife
My body felt weary and worn,
You always were near, to comfort and cheer
And you helped me to weather the storm.

I know you're waiting for me to come home
And I know just how long you've been gone,
But I never knew—until I lost you
Just how lonely I could be on my own.

How long will it be before I will see
Your beautiful face, free from pain,
From all burdens set free, no tears will there be
And your blue eyes will sparkle again.

A Soldier's Story

Andy Terry

The clouds that danced on the blue Virginia sky belied the storm that was raging within my soul. It would seem, at a glance, that all was well with the world as my family motored its way up I-95 toward Alexandria. But it wasn't. I was about to walk away from my wife and spend the next twelve months on the other side of the world. Each moment behind the wheel and each passing milepost seemed to indict me as we sped toward the railway station. I prayed that time would cease, that something . . . anything would come to intervene and prevent my leaving. But I was leaving, and nothing on earth, or above her painted countryside, would alter the events of the day.

In the "Kiss and Ride" lane, I stepped out of the car as Robin and the boys joined me. My emotions were approaching meltdown, but I had to maintain a veneer of composure. I kissed the guys and hugged them, then looked deep into the eyes of my best friend. "I'm sorry, Robin." My throat was totally bereft of moisture. We hugged and exchanged one more "I love you." With one more wave, I stepped onto the escalator that descended down to the platform. As my family faded from view, the emotions ripped forward in aching convulsions.

For the first fifteen years of our marriage, Robin and I were never apart for more than a few days, but this was something altogether different. Being a career military member, the prospect of separation had always stalked us from a distance. Each new assignment that maintained family unity brought a sigh or relief, knowing that we would "stay a family" for another three years. All of this changed one April morning when I was informed that I'd been selected for an unaccompanied remote tour to the Republic of Korea.

Immediately, I began to seek a way of escape. I prayed; I begged the intercession of others; I even tried to walk away from the military a few brief years short of retirement. However, all the doors of escape closed for a year.

I pondered the wisdom of God; I even questioned the love of God as the big jet arched across the Pacific. One thought remained clear; the love my wife and I shared would circle the globe.

The first days were the hardest of all. Of these, that first Sunday was the emotional low watermark. Of all the days of our week, Sunday was special. I would wake first to put the coffee on. Moments later Robin would stir from her sleep as the rich aroma of the freshly ground coffee laden with sweetened cream would waft into our room. In a sleepy voice with a smile that could paint the sky ablaze with one million sunrises, she'd say, "Mornin', Baby." After church we enjoyed our traditional Sunday meal of spaghetti and fresh bread.

That Sunday morning, however, there was nothing but the alarm clock mocking me. Chapel that morning seemed to be nothing more than a sterile religious exercise. A well-meaning soldier approached me to say, "So this is your first Sunday. Man, I guess you're really missing your family, huh?" The remark cut like a jagged shard of glass. It took every ounce of bearing and composure not to break down.

The ensuing days would pass somewhat easier, but the loneliness simply wouldn't be melted by the waning Korean autumn.

Each new day brought us one sunrise closer to our reunion. The winter came with little warning and was harder than what I'd come to know in Virginia. The winds that swept across the Korean peninsula seemed to chill me down to my soul. The loneliness was punctuated each morning as the alarm sounded at 6:00 A.M. I would awaken to an empty bed and a sterile room. Robin may well have resided in a neighboring galaxy, but love simply can't be snuffed out by mere geography. Just as my God chose to love me, I chose to love my wife. Each day this love grew stronger. It would not be shaken. Korean women would flirt, but their advances merely ricocheted off in harmless glancing blows.

On the forty-day point of our forced separation, a blessing arrived, borne on the backs of Korean movers. My computer arrived, and before that night was over, I was online chatting with Robin. This simple box, chocked full of silicon chips, became a "scarlet thread" that stretched halfway around the planet. Once again, mornings and evenings were spent with Robin. It was such a joy to log onto that Internet service and see her user name pop up on the screen. Her typed words painted the sky with newborn stars as she typed to me. These meetings would become a mainstay as I thanked God for allowing humanity to discover and develop computer technology. Every morning at 6:30 A.M. we were on for at least thirty minutes.

The weeknights provided for another good two hours, and the weekends were a marathon Internet session. Some Saturdays we spent up to eight hours together.

The Internet carried us through December, and it even allowed us to celebrate Christmas morning and New Year's Eve twice in one day. It was bittersweet togetherness. As we held time and space at bay, I longed for that sweet reunion that loomed somewhere beyond my horizon.

Spring came with little fanfare. Springtime has always been my favorite season. The fact that there were azalea bushes in Korea made spring all the more wonderful for me. The inland sea of the rice paddies slowly began to take on a green hue. The time of our reunion would soon be at hand, and my heart leapt with anticipation of crossing the globe, back to the arms of my beloved.

The day I'd longed for had arrived. The tears and pain of that day 220 days ago were all a distant memory.

The 747 lumbered down the long runway at Kimpo and suddenly lit off the ground as effortlessly as a sparrow. An eleven-hour flight across the Pacific is quite the journey for even the most seasoned fliers. I tried to sleep, but the excitement of the moment simply wouldn't allow it. Soon the California coast would only be seven miles beneath the wing of the mighty jet. Hours before, Robin and I were separated by the world's largest ocean. In a few moments, we would both be standing on the same continent. I let loose a silent prayer of thanksgiving for a safe flight as the giant aircraft rolled up to the arrival gate. Only one more flight now stood between the two of us.

The second flight was as smooth as crystal. The plane seemed to be suspended in a sea of diamonds with the stars above and the lights of cities below.

Finally, the jet slowed to begin its descent into the airspace above Washington. My thoughts were focused only on that sweet reunion. The plane simply couldn't land fast enough.

Off the plane, I made my way to the tram station that would take me from the arrival area to the main terminal of Dulles. The tram was full, but I managed to board first in order to be at its head when it would debark on the other side of the tarmac. Slowly, too slowly, this beast of burden lumbered across the half mile of asphalt that stood between me and the culmination of this journey. I spotted figures silhouetted in the window some two hundred yards ahead of me. It was her! I couldn't see the people; they were nothing more than dark, shadowy figures splashed against the flood of fluorescent light. But somehow, in my heart of hearts, I knew Robin and my boys were standing there. I could have been overwhelmed by the passionate daydreams of a soldier; yet all I felt was love, love like never before. The tram now positioned itself into a blind spot, and the beast lurched to a halt.

The doors opened, and we were greeted by a blast of cool air from the main terminal. With a sudden renewal of energy, I stepped off the tram and into the terminal. I was suddenly taken away by the beauty who was now right in front of me. Her radiance had the effect of one million supernovas igniting as one. Her smile would have jumped from her face and taken a life of its own had it been any bigger. Her eyes danced like two sapphires bathed in white light. Then she spoke; her two words soothed my weary soul. "Hi Andy." Her words seemed to arc like lightening into my very soul. *Where was the pain? What happened to the longing?* In a brilliant moment, they were exiled from this universe and sent to the netherworlds.

"Hi Sweetie," I replied. I dropped my knapsack and collapsed into her. Her perfume danced in my brain, and the softness of her hair gently caressed my face. Her embrace was tender, yet possessing a strength that seemed to well up from her soul. We kissed. For an eternal moment, we just took in one another. There was no Korea between us. In fact, my absence had vanished into nothing. The wife, the friend who had been wrenched from me, was now in my arms.

A Perfect Love Story

Bonnie Compton Hanson

Reading about a "Perfect Love Story" contest in the newspaper, I decided to enter. Rushing into my study, I flicked on my PC and reached for my keyboard. Suddenly, I heard, "Coo, coo."

I turned around. What in the world was that? I don't have a cuckoo clock. And my parakeets never made a sound like that.

Then all of a sudden, an almost imperceptible movement caught my eye, and I looked up. Sitting on top of my computer monitor was a beautiful young dove, her gray feathers glowing, her black eyes sparkling. Her head was cocked to one side as she watched me.

"Hello!" I exclaimed. What else does one say to a perfect stranger staring you in the face?

"Coo, coo. Coo-ah, coo, coo, coo!" she murmured softly. Then she fluffed her feathers and settled down for a nap.

Now, in case you're wondering, I didn't raise doves. My parakeets and cats kept me busy enough. All day long Blue Boy and Blue Belle filled my kitchen with their parakeet antics—billing and cooing, squabbling, and singing their hearts out. And they filled my nice clean floor with the perfectly good seeds they delighted in throwing from their cage.

Besides, this dove was wild, not one of those tame white ones used at weddings and such. This kind was well-equipped to leave messy little momentoes all over my house.

Thanks, but no thanks. "Shoo!" I shouted, reaching up to wave her away.

In reply, she simply moved over onto my hand and cocked her head again. "Coo, coo!"

"Look, Lovey," I replied, "you don't belong here, understand? Out, now, OUT!"

In the end, I had to carry her out myself. "Well, that's that!" I remarked as she flew to the large tree next door. Then I headed back to my "Perfect Love Story."

At lunchtime I grabbed a sandwich and sat down to watch the noon news.

Guess what? There was a gray dove sitting on my TV.

"Coo, coo. Coo-ah, coo, coo, coo," she murmured.

"You're sure a persistent one, aren't you, Lovey?" I asked, as I carefully escorted her back out. "It's not safe in my house. I have cats. Cats and birds don't mix. Now, out you go."

And she did leave—at least until the next morning. Taking a break from writing my "Perfect Love Story," I walked into the kitchen. As usual, the parakeets were having a seed-throwing contest. Pecking away on the floor at those same seeds was that chirpy little dove.

What if the cats saw her? Then I looked under the table. My cats were already there, staring at this strange new wonder. I couldn't take chances.

"All right, Lovey," I said, shooing her toward the door. "Out and stay out!"

She went as unhurriedly as she'd arrived, her graceful head bobbing as if to say, "Thanks for the lovely visit. See you later."

Even more remarkable, the cats stayed right where they were. They never tried to touch one shining feather!

After that, "Lovey" considered herself a part of the family. She'd eat her fill, then fly up to the fridge or into a bedroom or anywhere else in the house. Then she'd sit and preen her feathers with a soft, "Coo-ah, coo, coo, coo." Her favorite perching places were the TV (sometimes she'd lean over to watch the program upside down) and the garden window over my kitchen sink, snuggled among the pots of flowers. And our cats never gave her another thought.

I could have prevented all this, of course, by simply keeping my kitchen door closed. After all, we had a small cat door for the cats. But I loved the fresh spring air. Besides, I was getting as attached to this affectionate, perky bird as she was to her new home.

One day I saw her walking along our back patio—but not alone. A handsome male dove walked beside her. "Coo-ah, coo, coo, coo!" she murmured in his ear.

That's not what he was murmuring back! He was frantically trying to keep her away from such a dangerous place as our cat-filled house. She was just as determined not only to come in, but to have him come in with her!

Finally they seemed to agree on a compromise. She would come in and eat by herself, while he stood guard outside.

That became their daily schedule. He'd accompany her to her "favorite restaurant"; then she'd fly back with him to their new nest in the big tree next door. He was always so loving, faithful, and patient with her that we soon began calling him Dovey. Even though he never came inside, our cats accepted him as one of the family and left him quite alone.

Then one day Black Cat stopped by for a visit. Large, rangy, and ill-tempered, Black Cat was usually chased out of our yard as soon as our cats spotted him. On that day, however, none of our cats were around.

Suddenly I heard a terrified squawk. I rushed to the kitchen just in time to see Black Cat grab Lovey. Dovey began attacking him ferociously. Finally Black Cat let go and sulked off. Lovey was badly shaken up but had only lost a couple of feathers. As soon as she could, she and Dovey flew away to their tree in a chorus of dovetalk, "I told you so's!"

Though Lovey stayed away for a couple of days, she was soon back in our kitchen again, while Dovey unhappily paced our patio and kept an "eagle" eye on her. That's why he didn't see Black Cat until it was too late.

With a spring, the huge cat landed right on Dovey. Screaming, Lovey rushed to his defense, with me right behind her. We were too late though. Black Cat had bitten right through that courageous little heart. Dovey was dead.

For days afterward, I could hear Lovey's mournful cry from her lonely tree, though she never came near our house again. The next week our neighbors chopped the tree down; and Lovey was gone forever.

I finally had time to complete my "Perfect Love Story." I crumbled up the sheets I'd written and threw them away. No love I could imagine could compare with the one I had witnessed. So, Lovey and Dovey, this is for you—your own "Perfect Love Story."

16
Romance-Wise

Love is friendship set on fire.
Jeremy Taylor

The Last Rose of Summer

Don Haines

We have a rosebush growing by the side of our house. Sheila planted it many years ago when we were young. She loves all her plants and flowers, but this rosebush is special; it represents our marriage.

During our early years of our marriage, I'd celebrate some special occasion by sending Sheila a dozen red roses from a local florist. I thought I was being romantic by sending my lady something she really loved. But I never got the reaction I wanted. She'd thank me, place them on the mantle, and say, "They're beautiful, but they won't last long." It would be a long time before I would understand what she was trying to tell me.

Those roses on the mantle bloomed for a while, but they'd been mortally wounded. Sheila knew there was nothing she could do to give them life. No matter what she did, they would slowly fade and die. As beautiful as they were, they were only temporary.

Unlike the cut roses, Sheila nurtured our rosebush, just as she's nurtured our marriage—with tender loving care—because that's what it takes.

No matter how dead things seem, love can burst out of its dormant state—like roses in the spring. If two people work at keeping love alive, like the rosebush, love will always renew itself.

Sheila has patiently put up with the winters of our relationship and waited for spring. Through her effort, unlike the dozen roses on our mantle, our marriage has suffered no mortal wounds. And now, as we approach the autumn of our lives, I'm finally the person she envisioned when she married me over forty years ago.

As the warmth of summer chills to deep autumn, there are only two roses left. The bush itself is turning brown, getting ready to sleep for the winter. A few moments ago, we stood together in our yard, looking at the rosebush that has shared our life. "It will be winter soon," Sheila said. "There are only two roses left."

I smiled. "But it will be as pretty as ever in the spring. It always is."

Reflections on Love

Linda Karges-Bone

In my freshman level education course, Principles of American Education, known in university life as Ed. 2-01, I begin the semester by inviting the students to write me a letter. They can say anything they wish in the letter, but for a start, I want to know about their roots, their desire to become teachers, and why they chose Charleston Southern University.

Recently, a shy, twenty-two-year-old youth ministry student from upstate wrote that he had gotten married during the summer and that he thanked God for his "perfect marriage." Continuing, the satisfied newlywed stated, "We never argue and seem to agree on every matter. Marriage is so much easier than I thought it would be."

As I read the letter while sitting in my den, a basket of laundry overflowed at my feet. My children quarreled over whose turn it was to feed the beagle, and my husband's irksome voice lurked behind the blinking red light on the answering machine, threatening, "I hope we're having something good for dinner tonight . . . not something made out of that bag of ten thousand skinless, boneless, tasteless chicken breasts we bought at the wholesale shopping club . . ." I couldn't help but laugh out loud and think, *Enjoy the honeymoon while you can, Sweetie. Things only get tougher from here on out!*

I have learned that disappointments in marriage can give your relationship substance and integrity.

Early in my marriage, I was disappointed when my husband did not want to spend every waking moment with me.

"You don't love me," I would accuse.

"Just don't hang on me so much; I can't breathe," he would retort.

Not good. Not healthy. Big disappointment for both of us.

However, I learned to seek out my own friendships and interests, going out to dinner on occasion with some teacher friends and eventually teaching a water aerobics class. Pursuing my master's and doctoral degrees also figured into my sense of self-fulfillment.

All of these pursuits and a growing maturity strengthened our marriage. Just yesterday, my husband of twenty years and I hooked up to sample one of the new "stir fries" for lunch at Shoney's.

Over a lively lunch, he said, "I'm glad you're not boring like Frank's wife. She always seems so depressed and unhappy."

"I like my life," I said with a smile. And I do. My marriage is important. It, along with my faith, form the core of who I am and what I do, but I'm still me.

Disappointment in marriage? Inevitable. Destruction to romance? Not a chance if you believe that God has given you a marvelous gift in the person of your spouse! Now, what about those chicken breasts? Pot pie? Stir fry? Perhaps the dreaded pilaf that he especially dislikes? What will I try? That depends on my sense of humor and goodwill. After all, the preacher never mentioned, "Avoid culinary boredom," in the sentence with "love, honor, and cherish."

A Special Couple

Carolyn Scheidies

A special couple still loving,
An increasingly rare and beautiful thing.
Two walking life's pathway together,
Not parted by anything.
Walking together hand in hand,
From gentle spring through winter's blast.
A relationship bonded by God's love,
Is the only kind that lasts.
For he is the author of caring,
Of commitment which never ends.
Bonding two hearts together,
Still lovers, companions, and friends.

Romance in the Park

Heidi S. Hess

Thirty-something years of singleness can add up to a lot of dates—some more forgettable than others. One of those dates, though, will always be one of the richest gems in my memory bank. It was the day I decided my now husband was "the one." (If you asked Craig what sealed the deal for him, he would probably say something about my lemon tarts. But I digress.)

Let me tell you about our second date, on June 6, 1998.

I first noticed Craig at the University of Michigan Ballroom Dance Club. He was a big guy, and yet he danced with a confidence and grace that belied his size. One day he waltzed over to me (literally) and asked me out to dinner, then after dinner asked if he could see me again. I agreed to a picnic in the park with him and my precocious border collie, Missy.

Craig picked me up around noon, dressed to impress and armed with flowers and a picnic from Boston Market. More impressed with the chicken sandwiches than the miniature carnations, Missy followed close behind on her leash with her favorite neon-pink plastic ball protruding from her mouth.

This particular park has a river running through it, with Japanese-style bridges arching about twelve feet over the water. As we sat by the side of the river, eating and talking, Craig alternately bit into his sandwich and threw the ball into the water for Missy to retrieve. She hadn't learned to swim yet, and so would wade in only up to her undercarriage. After the third toss, the ball hit the water a few feet beyond her reach, so Missy just looked back at us as if to say, "So now what do I do?" Meanwhile, the ball bobbed farther and farther downstream.

Rushing to the rescue, Craig stripped off his socks and shoes, rolled up his pant legs, and jumped into the murky river up to his waist! Once he was back up on the riverbank, he nonchalantly handed the ball to Missy, and we packed up the rest of our picnic and squished back to the car. I was hugely impressed with Craig at this point, but apparently Missy thought a retest was in order. So, when we reached the top of the bridge, Missy spit the ball back into the water, then looked at Craig as if to say, "OK, ya gonna get that one too?"

At that moment I marveled at his self-control. Instead of tossing Missy into the river after the ball, Craig mildly observed, "Well, don't think we'll be able to salvage that one." But the next time he came to the house, he had a new pink ball in hand for my "problem child."

If you ask twenty women what qualities they look for in a man, you'll get twenty different answers: strong, brave, dependable, handsome, wealthy. Me? If I ever have a daughter, I'll be sure to give her my secret: "Hold out for the one who makes a good impression on your dog."

Do Ya Think I'm Sexy?

Nancy Kennedy

He wasn't supposed to laugh. It was in the early days of our marriage and I wanted to try something—well—different. I'd read a book that said if I did this one thing I'd put a smile on my husband's face that would last all week, or something like that. So I tried it. I wrapped myself in plastic wrap. Naked.

When my unsuspecting husband came in from his Saturday softball game and beheld me in all my Saran-wrapped splendor, he smiled all right. He laughed, threw back his head, and roared. Called me a nut. Couldn't get over what a joker I was. Then he turned on the television while I peeled myself in the bathroom and cried.

Next I tried a pale pink satin nightie with spaghetti straps. As Barry locked the front door for the night, I disappeared into the bathroom to change and make my grand entrance. I slunk into the bedroom, a seductive tigress in pink. That's when I discovered my husband has an aversion to slick fabric. He's afraid his rough, mechanic's hands will snag it. But he didn't tell me then. He just kissed me on the cheek and kept his distance while I stared into the darkness, wondering whether I was sexy.

Later I went back to climbing into bed wearing his old hockey jersey and wool socks, and, well . . .

Flash forward a few years and two babies later. I step out of the shower and catch a glimpse of myself in the full-length mirror. I have a belly that I can tuck into the back pocket of my jeans and sagging breasts that rival those of any African tribal mama you see pictured in *National Geographic*. Before I can hide myself in a towel, my husband barges into the bathroom. He whistles appreciatively. I tell him he's nuts.

Later I'm doing the dishes, wearing my favorite old jeans and huge blue sweater that hangs down to my knees. Barry comes up behind me and purrs, "You are so sexy!"

Which brings me to the question: What is sexy? If you believe what you see on television and the pages of fashion magazines, sexiness is perceived perfection, air-brushed flawlessness. It's sultry looks, salacious murmurings, and bodies that defy gravity. It's six-pack abs, perfect pecs, and full, pouty lips reserved for "Baywatch" babes and "Melrose Place" beauties.

If you ask my husband, however, he'll give you a different answer. Barry has this thing for actress Gillian Anderson, Agent Scully on "The X-Files." "She's just a basic, beautiful woman," he told me one day. That's when I asked him what he finds sexy about me.

"Your green eyes drive me wild," he said. "And your smile. You're like Scully—just basic, nothing fancy or fake. Besides, I love you, and that's what makes you sexy to me."

Likewise, when I consider Barry's sexiness, the crinkly lines around his eyes top my list along with his muscular arms. But even sexier is the way he knows his way around Home Depot and his knowledge of pipe joints and sheet metal ducts. What's appealing goes beyond what he looks like. It's more about who he is, his competence, and the security I have in knowing he cares for me.

My Sweet Gum Miracle

D. J. Note

I struggled to dig two holes in the black soil on either side of our barnyard gate. Salty beads of perspiration trickled down the side of my face. For months my husband neglected to plant my sweet gum trees as he had promised. One tree still appeared healthy, but the second had succumbed to the confines of its tiny bucket. As I lifted the lifeless little trunk from the container, the last tentacles of root tore away. *If only he had kept his promise,* I thought, shoving the dehydrated stump into the hole. I pushed the dirt up around the tree covering its base with the suffocating sticky soil. Secretly I hoped guilt would overcome my husband when he saw the dead tree. A reminder of his unkept promise.

For nearly a month, I watered and pampered the remaining tree, completely ignoring the dried torso sticking out of the ground on the opposite end of the gate. Then one day I noticed tiny, bright-green foliage clinging to the base of the dead tree's trunk. My mind struggled to believe what my eyes couldn't deny. Without fanfare, God had resurrected the lifeless tree. And without water! I threw my arms into the air in grateful worship, but just as suddenly, I felt utterly humbled. Until now, the bitterness I felt toward my husband for his unkept promise had consumed me. I felt small and ashamed, like Adam and Eve must have felt in the garden when they tried to run and hide. In spite of my anger, God was demonstrating his love for me. It was the first time I realized that God truly cares about even the small, insignificant things in my life. And he's bigger than all my frustrations and fear. "Oh Father, forgive me," I whispered. "I've been so angry."

Over the next few months, I cared for both trees. As the tiny resurrected tree flourished, the other healthy tree slowly withered and, despite all my efforts, died. Then one day, in the quiet of my mind, I recognized his voice. *Man's labors will vanish, but that which I bring for you is sustained.*

I didn't replant another tree in place of the one that died—not as a memorial to my husband's broken promise, but this time as a reminder to me of my own lack of forgiveness. And our twenty-foot sweet gum tree thrives today, a testimony to us both of God's unfailing mercy and love.

How to be Sexy

Karl Forehand

My wife remarked one day, "You know what I think is sexy?" I have to admit that she had my undivided attention. (I had been wondering that for years.) She said, "It's sexy when you spend time with the kids playing games and things like that."

I don't have to tell you what my response to that was. I immediately called out to my son, "Jordan, get in here; we're going to play some Uno, right now!"

Romance is very elusive, especially to men. We try to be romantic, but it seems to always be just beyond our grasp. We think we know what's involved, but we don't have a clue.

Another clue came after our third child was born. My mother-in-law was in town, and she fixed dinner for us. After dinner, on a whim, I cleaned up the dishes and cleared the table. Well, this surprisingly brought my wife to tears, and she exclaimed, "I'm starting to have those feelings again!"

I might add that I was pretty lazy most of the day, not helping much at all, but I did step in when I knew she would appreciate it most.

The reason, I think, that my wife loves those little things is because it shows that I care enough to be attentive to her needs. I didn't have to do all the housework; I just had to be sensitive and attentive enough to notice what to do when she did need help.

As I thought about it, I probably appreciate the same things from her. I never expect her to keep the house spotless, but when I'm engrossed in something on the computer, she might walk up and offer to get me a cup of coffee. She doesn't say, "Could I indenture myself to you as a life long servant?" She just offers to do something nice that makes my life more comfortable.

Timing is key, and if your spouse has to ask you to do it, you've lost the effectiveness. Caring enough to be attentive pays big dividends. After all, it's not how you look that makes you sexy. Sexiness is found in sweet considerations given to one another in love.

17
Romance Restored

Love is like fresh bread.
It has to be remade all the time, made new.

Ursula K. LeGuin

When a Soul Waits

Jan Johnson

As the clock struck midnight, all the couples at the New Year's Eve party kissed, except Greg and me. Finally, my friend said, "Come on, Greg, give your wife a kiss." So Greg gave me a token peck. I trembled at this first physical contact in years, but I tried to act as if it were nothing. After all, it was nothing but a socially conventional behavior forced by circumstances.

Three years before, my husband Greg told me that he hated me and planned to leave. I sat quietly as he listed for me the offenses I had committed. At one point, he produced a list of ten criticisms I'd launched on him within one hour before work one morning. I couldn't defend myself.

He was right.

I asked Greg to forgive me, and I worked very hard to change. I read self-help books, held in my anger until my eyes crossed, and finally landed in a support group. There I talked about the rage that had grown within me since childhood, and I became accountable for my critical behavior. I spent hours crying out to God, asking him to help me change.

During the next two years, I changed dramatically. Greg admitted as much and consented to see a counselor. It was there he said, "I no longer hate her. Now I feel absolutely nothing."

After working with us for a while, the counselor said, "I can't do anything else for you two until Greg decides he wants to reawaken his feelings."

"I haven't decided that," Greg replied.

I felt even more alone. I could imagine how I looked from miles out in the atmosphere: one person completely alone casting a long shadow behind myself. It was just God and me now. I berated myself; I cried many times a day; I stared at oncoming trains at railroad crossings and imagined pulling out in front of the engine.

Greg didn't have the energy to leave, he said. He thought I would, but I couldn't because I wanted to stand before God on judgment day with my marriage intact. Part of that was a desire to obey God, and another part was pride. I felt like such a second-class person for having a dead marriage.

I also wanted to save my kids from the pain of divorce. I figured we could fake it until the kids grew up. We no longer argued; we didn't talk much at all. I also stayed because I loved Greg. I didn't realize what a patient, generous person he was until the day he confronted me, and I was charmed by him.

My darkest reason for staying was that I feared abandonment. Having someone who didn't notice me was better than having no one at all. I wasn't sure I could get up in the morning without someone to lean on, however tenuously. Every time he was late from work, I imagined he'd taken off for Mexico.

I felt jealous of other married couples who argued all the time but still professed their love for each other. We never argued; we never loved. How would I survive a hopeless marriage?

At the beginning of this long waiting room, I read stories about marriages that turned around in an evening, a month, or a year. I wanted this to happen to us, so every few months I asked Greg if his feelings had returned yet. He felt inadequate, saying, "I'd like to change my feelings, but I can't."

His words, "I can't," rang in my ears. I was helpless too. I couldn't change his mind. I could do nothing but wait. In the meantime, the pain was terrible. *What was I going to do about me now that no one loved me?*

One by one, I found avenues of God's love that made him more real to me than ever before. The songs at the new church we attended spoke of God's love for a discarded person like me. I wept through the services for months.

My support group demonstrated God's unconditional love each time I confessed my fierce anger to the group. I looked up expecting to see condemning faces, but instead I saw gentle smiles and nodding heads accepting me and my rage. Their faces became the loving face of God for me so that I muttered Romans 5:8 many times a day: "While we were yet sinners, Christ died for us." I began to believe that God loved me as much on the days I hated myself and the world as he did on the days when I was cheery and sweet.

In solitude, I cried out to God. I walked through a nearby cemetery, screaming out those painful, unexplainable Psalms David groaned in the night and drowned his bed with tears. I lay down next to tombstones and grieved for God to come inside me and convince every cell in my body that he loved me. I cried in the shower as I leaned against the wall tiles, asking God to rescue me from my regret, self-pity, and self-hate. I scribbled my own angry, grieving psalms in my journal, saying abominable, hateful things about Greg, and then asking for blessing on this beautiful man I loved. Little by little, I began to believe that God loved me in my ugliest moments and walked with me each minute.

In the safety of these moments, I faced the fact that Greg's heart might never change. Over and over I surrendered my dreams of reconciliation. With God's love as the only basis for self-worth, I decided I could face living the rest of my life in a relationship where I was not loved. I could be obedient to God and stay in my marriage with no guarantee that anything would ever improve. Occasionally, I got on my high horse (*I deserve something better!*), but then I gave the marriage back to God again. The changes I had made in surrendering my anger and manipulative ways were helping me in every area of life so that one day I wrote: "I have changed to please you, God, not Greg. Even if he never changes, I'll still be glad I did."

As I sensed God's companionship, I took delight in giving to Greg without trying to change his mind or make him like me again. It was a grand experiment to try to love him and leave his freedom intact.

We sat in this waiting room of surrender for several years. Some would say they were wasted years, but even marriages that offer little to brag about can be of great value. We helped and respected each other like brother and sister. We loved our children. We reached out to friends and neighbors. My imperfect marriage did not make me a hopeless and unworthy Christian.

Those years of dry desert gave Greg room to work through his feelings so he could learn to enjoy the new person I had become. We eased into reconciliation so slowly that I didn't know it was happening. Finally, one day on the telephone, Greg said, "I love you," just before he hung up. Stunned, I almost said, "Are you sure?"

My story cannot be reduced to a formula. I never viewed my willingness to wait as a way of earning Greg's love back. It could have gone the other way. We were both ripe for affairs, and that's what usually happens in these cases.

Only by God's grace did I understand that I had expected Greg to meet the inner needs only God could meet. Greg couldn't give me the unrelenting attention I needed; he couldn't assure me that I was a valuable person; he couldn't wash away my mistakes. Only God can do those things. In the rawest edges of life, I find the courage to face each day as I believe in my heart that God loves me no matter what.

Love's Blanket

S. F. Peacock

Two children within two years of marriage, and the two of us were in trouble. Though our children were beautiful, healthy, and active, we were often tired, grumpy, and snippy.

Our mood became increasingly depressed as we worked to make a home on a very limited income. Our energy and time stretched to meet the needs of a growing family. Soon my husband and I lost touch with each other.

Conversations between us, when they did occur, were short and precise. Fortunately, hostility or meanness did not factor into our relationship. Blame for our mutual lack of caring for the other remained locked away. There simply was no emotion, no feeling of any kind. We were dull to each other. Once humor and laughter were commonplace in everything we did and said; now our giggles were replaced with sadness.

The worst, the very worst part of living together was going to bed. Before our lives became sad, we never went to bed without wishing the other sweet dreams or sharing a good-night kiss.

We found more solace and comfort in our electric blanket than we did in each other's arms. With duel controls, we could dial the amount of warmth we needed and required. Night after night I would set my dial to medium and remember how he used to tease me, "You're one hot lady, Love."

Then he would lightly touch the bare of my back and whisper in my ear, "Sssssssss." He would quickly move his hand as if he had touched a hot iron as we played and loved. A favorite joke of his was to tell our close friends that I was a natural electric blanket because I was always warm to his touch. "What we need," he would tell them, "is a refrigerator blanket for the summer because my wife is simply too hot to handle."

Now his hand only touched the blanket controls as he set his dial to low.

One particularly cold winter night I went to bed first, which had become our custom. Later, after the late news show, my husband came to bed. There was no good-night kiss, no wish for sweet dreams. There was no "I love you," from him. I, in turn, offered no murmurs to him. Turning toward the wall, I closed my eyes, knowing that sleep would once again be difficult to find.

That night the wind seemed to blow through every closed window in our bedroom. It was not long before I reached over and increased the temperature on my half of the blanket. The storm raged on, and soon I heard him reach over to adjust his controls.

Later I awoke and found our poor room in a deep freeze. I turned the heat of the blanket to hot and pulled the blanket tighter around me. In the past, we would snuggle whenever it was cold. I loved to snuggle. We would snuggle on the couch in the evening as we watched TV, and later we would snuggle in the bed. I was thinking of that when I felt him get out of bed. To my amazement, he went to one of the drafty windows and opened it. "What are you doing?" I asked incredulously.

Startled, he answered, "Letting in some air. It's hot in here."

"No it's not. I'm freezing." Turning on my table lamp, I continued, "I can't turn the controls up any higher. Please close the window."

"But I'm too hot. I've turned my side completely off and I'm still . . ."

Like a cold blast of fresh air, more than one window opened that night. We looked at each other and started to laugh. We hadn't laughed so hard in months. My blanket control was on his side of the bed, and his control was on mine. Together we unraveled the controls to the electric blanket.

In doing so, his hand touched mine. It was not so long before that he used to touch me a lot. And, it felt good.

I climbed into bed and adjusted the controls, setting the dial to medium.

"Do we need this?" he asked. He was still standing at the foot of the bed.

"Need what?"

"Do we need this electric blanket?"

"Not really." I wasn't sure what he meant.

"Good." He pulled the bedspread off. Then he threw the electric blanket with its wires and controls into a pile in the corner of our room. I pulled an old blanket from the closet, and together we remade the bed.

Back in bed, I watched him staring up at the ceiling. Finally he said, "As I remember, you're warmer than any blanket."

Not knowing what to say and afraid that I would say the wrong thing, I replied, "That's what you've always told me."

He was quiet for a while. "I guess I haven't said much to you lately. I guess I felt that I didn't have much of anything worthwhile to say to you."

"You can tell me anything," I told him. It was true. I wanted him to tell me everything. I was tired of living this way.

Placing a rather cool hand on the bare of my back brought back my sense of belonging. Face to face, he told me he was sorry for the way he had been acting. Since our second child came into our lives, he had been worried about how he could afford to feed, to house, and to clothe us on his salary. Worry and embarrassment left him depressed and afraid of tomorrow.

I was so happy he had told me his worries. When my turn came, I apologized for my grumpy moods, lack of kind words, and suspicions. Caring for the children ran me ragged, leaving me short-tempered and short of humor.

That night I told him why I married him, why I had his children, and why I loved him. I told him that where we lived and what things we owned did not mean as much as being a family whose members talked to each other and had fun being together.

That night he promised to help more with the care and raising of the children. More importantly, he promised to include me in his life.

That night we renewed our love for each other.

Since then, we've had a third child, moved a couple of times, and have never gone to sleep without a good-night kiss and a wish for sweet dreams. As for the electric blanket with dual controls, I stored it for years and finally sold it in a garage sale. With the money we made, we treated the entire family to a loving conversation over ice cream.

Beneath the Rain-Spattered Dirt

Connie Neal

Something about the brisk chill in the air, the first scent of smoke from family-room fireplaces, and colorful leaves whispering their way to the ground struck me with a sudden urgency.

"It's fall!" I called to my husband Patrick as I leaped from the car, "It's time to plant tulip bulbs!"

He looked up, dusting the dirt from his hands, "Aren't you even going to say hello?"

I'd been gone for the weekend, speaking at a retreat.

"Hon, I'll go buy bulbs. You're already working in the yard." I'd missed my chance to plant bulbs the two previous years, leaving me to envy my neighbor's tulips. I'd vowed not to let that happen again.

"Surely, you're tired! Aren't you?" he reasoned, but my mind was set. If impulsiveness were a virtue, I could be canonized as a saint. His reasonable protests gave way to a smile.

"You don't even let me surprise you."

"What?"

He pointed to the corner flower bed. "You see this dirt? I spent all weekend turning it into fertile soil. Hidden beneath it are tulips and hyacinths."

He pointed to the flower bed around our small tree. "Over there—come springtime—you'll have more daffodils than you can count." (He knows how I love daffodils!) "And under the front window, ranunculus of every color."

Ranunculus! I could imagine them on their solitary stems like a corps of ballerinas dancing in the breeze.

His smile held a touch of tenderness, "I just wanted to surprise you."

The dirt before us had not changed, but its meaning had. Our marriage had been severely tested eight years before, leaving me prone to momentary bouts of insecurity. That winter a fiery dart of fear pierced my heart, and I cried out to the Lord for help.

God reminded me, "Connie, you have tulips hidden in your flower bed."

I didn't understand until I recalled that tulips are a symbol of love and devotion. My husband hadn't given me a bouquet—here today, gone next week. He'd hidden bulbs beneath the dirt. That meant he intended to stay with me through the winter when all we could see was the rain-spattered dirt. He planned to be there in the spring to share my joy and year after year to see the blooms return in greater glory.

Oh, what a glorious springtime that was! I spread my blanket in the yard, surrounded by the colorful display of my husband's love and devotion. It was beautiful!

The Big Squeeze

Paul Kortepeter

Forget fancy restaurants. Jenny and I couldn't afford the burger joint down the block. And forget expensive lingerie. We were lucky to have matching socks.

As economically challenged newlyweds, we relied on a lowly candle to spark a romantic evening. Actually, it only took one candle to light our tiny apartment.

In the shadows, we could forget that our kitchen was the size of a closet, that our closet was brimming with junk, and that our knees hit the sink every time we used the commode. We could forget that our refrigerator barely held a jug of milk and that we didn't own a TV or a stereo. In the shadows, we could kick back on our futon sofa (which doubled as our bed) and feel like millionaires in a resort hotel.

But the romantic spell was frequently broken by the rabble-rousers who surrounded our small paradise. The leather-clad actress living next door blasted heavy metal music all hours of the night. In the apartment on the opposite side, a Michael Jackson impersonator played the "Thriller" album over and over, vigorously wailing along while he took three-hour showers.

Even worse were the neighbors across the alley— two Valley girls who constantly chattered about cosmetics, their therapists, and alternative medicine. In case you had any doubt, this was Los Angeles.

At times our neighbors' weird habits got to us. "We never have any privacy," I complained. "We're like goldfish stuck in a bowl." I turned around and saw one of the Valley girls staring at me sourly across the narrow alley.

"You guys are so neurotic," she snapped and slammed her window shut.

We tried to entertain friends, but even that sometimes made us feel poor. "Wow, you two must really like each other," they would exclaim upon entering our living room/dining room/bedroom. Hastily we'd turn off the lights and get out the ambiance candle. Surely our guests couldn't fail to notice how lovely everything looked in the dark.

A less-than-subtle visitor once said, "No offense, but I'd go insane after a week here. How do you guys do it?"

How did we do it?

We were creative. We took long walks around our neighborhood, rain or shine. We played smash ball in the park. We created exotic milkshakes in our blender. We toured art museums that offered free admission. We drove to the mountains and gazed at the lights of the city. In those days of scarcity, we really got to know each other. We couldn't help it.

One particular night combined the highs and lows of our first year together. Jenny and I were furious with each other, but we didn't want to start yelling because the neighbors would listen in. As for stomping outside to cool down, it was too late for either of us to be roaming the streets of L.A.

Jenny tried to hole up in the bathroom, but five minutes later she emerged. "I can't even sulk properly in there," she complained. "It's too cramped."

"It's not too cramped for me," I snapped. I closed the door and took a seat on the throne, slamming my knees against the sink. It was only five minutes before I re-emerged.

"We can't get away from each other," Jenny groaned. "We don't have any room to breathe. It's like . . . it's like . . ."

"It's like we're married," I finished her sentence.

"Yeah," she sighed.

We stared at each other, confounded by the permanence of it all.

Just then the room started shaking. Our closet doors burst open, and junk flooded the room. Plaster dropped from the ceiling. Jenny ran for cover under the front door frame. I dived into the closet. As the world convulsed, we exchanged frightened looks.

"I love you!" Jenny shouted.

"I love you too!" I answered.

The earthquake was over in a few seconds, but afterward, when the dust had settled, we both felt very rich indeed.

The Unexpected Messenger

Dayle Allen Shockley

On a brisk day in April, my husband and I stood in the middle of the living room floor, arguing. We seemed to be doing little else lately. I don't recall what started the whole thing; probably something as insignificant as who left the closet lights on. Still, I rambled on, making little, if any, sense. My husband's face remained a picture of sheer frustration.

At last I announced with great emphasis, "I'm getting out of here!"

"Go," Stan said, shrugging his broad shoulders. "Do whatever you want to do." He turned and walked away.

Still muttering, I stomped to the pantry, grabbed an old loaf of bread, stalked to the car, and drove to the duck pond.

This particular duck pond sits twelve miles from our home in the center of the cemetery where my father-in-law is buried. For some reason, the pond had been a compass to me during difficult times. Maybe it held an answer today.

A parade of squawking ducks waddled to greet me. While I reached into the back seat for my sweater and the things I'd brought, they nosed around my feet, searching for whatever treats they could find.

"Just old bread, you guys," I said, shooing them out of the way.

The entire congregation trailed me to the small cement bench next to the pond. Hungrily, they eyed me as

I unwrapped my meager offering. In minutes the crumbs were consumed, and I silently enjoyed the pleasant breeze as the ducks sashayed off in every direction.

For a while, I sat under the Texas pines thinking about the argument I'd walked out on. All my life I'd heard that the seventh year of marriage was the toughest; that men and women often contracted the seven-year itch or something similar. I dared not define my own ailment, except to acknowledge that my marriage had tarnished over the years. The reasons varied, but my tendency to drone on when enough had been said didn't help matters. I always wanted to have the last word—at any cost.

Often I vowed to be different, spending weeks with Ecclesiastes 3:7—*a time to be silent and a time to speak* (NIV)—taped on my bathroom mirror. Before long, I'd find myself stuck in the same old rut again; talking when silence was in order. Inwardly, I longed for change.

Getting up from where I sat, I strolled to the edge of the pond, watching the ducks in the water creating spectacular silver circles around them, their reflections a kaleidoscope of colors.

If only I could behold my own reflection like the ducks in the water, I thought. *If only I could see myself.* And so I breathed a silent prayer, asking God to let this miraculous thing happen.

It was while I prayed that a car approached the little pond. Stopping a dozen feet from where I stood, the engine sputtered a time or two, then died. Turning, I saw an elderly man crawling out of an ancient, ramshackle Cadillac, the vinyl roof peeling off in great chunks.

Tall and lean, the man moved briskly around the front of the car, swinging two loaves of white Wonder bread in his hands. He wore a red flannel shirt with sleeves clasped at the wrist and jean britches that were about an inch too short.

Hurriedly, he laid the bags of bread on the hood of the Cadillac, opened them, and began flinging whole slices through the dazzling sun like tiny white Frisbees.

"You come here often?" I called out across the grass. He cupped a hand to one ear.

"Do you come here often?" I said a bit louder.

Tossing the final slices, he stuffed the plastic wrappers in a garbage bin and walked to where I now sat on the bench.

"I'm sorry, ma'am," he said, squatting beside me. "I still didn't hear you."

"I just wanted to know if you come here often," I said, suddenly wishing I hadn't said anything.

"I come when the weather's nice," he said. I found it unnerving that he did not look directly into my eyes when he spoke but stared curiously at my forehead.

For nothing better to do, we sat together on the bench. A cluster of ducks gathered at our feet and honked at a lofty volume. So loud was their honking that I had to resist the urge to jump up and yell, "SHHHH!" at the top of my lungs.

I glanced at the old man. He smiled but said nothing. I wished he would leave.

As if reading my mind, the man sprang to his feet and said, "I gotta split." Then he pointed a bony finger at the chattering ducks, and in an irked voice said, "You know, them crazy ducks just don't know when to hush."

With that declaration—and a wave in my direction—the old man sauntered to the waiting jalopy, brought it to life, and clanked off in the distance, a flurry of leaves chasing after him.

With a bewildered face, I stared at the disappearing car. What did he say? Suddenly, it seemed like a light bulb turned on in my head. *Did he say those crazy ducks just don't know when to hush?*

At once, I recalled my prayer, my desire to see myself. *Did God propel me to this place to catch a unique glimpse of myself?* I wondered. *Did I sound much like the honking ducks?* Suddenly, I knew I did, and I had the uncanny feeling that I had just entertained an angel.

Turning abruptly, I hurried to the car, a gust of April's wind whipping around my legs. The little ducks stood quietly now, like tiny monuments scattered across the ground. Their silence spoke volumes to me.

When I arrived home, my husband lay sprawled on the couch, looking worried. "Hi," he said, his voice even. "Where've you been?"

I hesitated briefly. "I went to the cemetery."

"Cemetery!" He half laughed. "Are you planning on killing me?"

"Nope," I said, planting a kiss on his puzzled face, "but I got some great pointers on keeping you alive."

Memory Quilt

Linda Evans Shepherd

(continued . . .)

The aroma of roasted turkey still lingered, mixed with whiffs of chocolate-raspberry coffee and traces of pumpkin pie. Bonnie and I settled into the soft blue and rose floral cushions of the living room sofa. We could hear happy shrieks of my young son and her two children echoing through the house as they played a game of chase. Our husbands were somewhere beneath our feet, in Paul's basement office, toying with his computer.

I sighed deeply, content that this Thanksgiving Day was at a most peaceful end. Memories of preceding Thanksgivings pieced themselves together in my mind's eye. Some came in pleasant, eye-pleasing patterns . . .

I stared at the small purple wheelchair that stood in the corner. Some memories only darkened the past.

Shuddering off my remembered grief, I pulled my Scripture-stitched quilt over my lap and turned to study my friend, Bonnie. I thought of our twenty-year friendship that had trailed from the halls of a Texas high school to two separate Texas universities and finally landing in nearby Colorado towns.

"Linda," Bonnie confided in hushed tones, breaking through my daydreams. "I have something I want to tell you—something I haven't told anyone else."

"What's that?" I asked with a yawn.

Bonnie said, "Steve and I are getting a divorce."

The news snipped remnants of time into layered patches. Fifteen years unraveled, and I remembered a much younger Steve, a Steve who came bounding across the university campus to where Paul, my then boyfriend, and I sat on a green carpet of grass beneath a shady oak.

"I met the most wonderful girl," Steve said with a grin. "We're going to get married!"

"Who is it?" I asked, standing.

"Bonnie Loran," he announced.

"Bonnie!" I gave him a hug. "I'm so happy for you!"

Later, when Paul and I were newlyweds and enrolled in a north Texas graduate school, Steve and Bonnie lived a few blocks away. We often celebrated holidays with husband-blackened barbecues in the park.

I remembered when Steve and Bonnie followed us to Colorado in a move to nearby Greeley. Bonnie had dropped out of college to take care of their babies, who were two years apart, while Steve studied for his doctorate. The love was thick in their tiny trailer despite the dresser-drawer nursery and the master bedroom on a fold-out couch.

I remembered how Steve and Bonnie had been there for Paul and me when our daughter had been in a car accident that left her severely disabled.

My eyes blinked hard, and I reached for Bonnie who had shrunk into the cushions. "What happened?" I asked, grief-stricken.

"Steve is dating one of my best friends."

The impact of Steve's betrayal tossed my dreams into nightmares. The ripping apart of the fabric of

Bonnie's life seemed to rend my own. Repeatedly, I'd dream that Paul would announce he had a new girlfriend and I had to move out of our home. I became cross with Paul, snapping at him at the slightest provocation.

My night-time nightmares were compounded by real life. Bonnie and the kids moved in with us for two weeks while she tried to decide what to do.

Later, she said, "Steve's betrayal has been more devastating than if he had died. In one blow I've lost my in-laws, my friends, and my church. It's like my whole life, memories included, has been devoured by a tornado."

I felt like I was in a tornado, too, as four more dear friends plunged into the divorce process.

One night Paul and I sat down together to talk.

"Why have you been so upset lately?" he asked.

"I'm sorry," I said. "All these divorces are really getting to me. I can't help but recall the happy times we all spent together. Now we will never be able to share time with these couples again."

Paul sighed. "It's really sad; isn't it?"

I nodded my agreement. "I just don't understand why our friends want to throw away their past."

Later this question haunted my thoughts as I helped another divorced friend pick through nineteen years worth of scrapped accumulation from her first marriage.

"I don't want any of it," Vicki had said. "I have a new life now, a new love. All this old stuff just reminds me of Bill, and I don't want to think of him anymore. You can take whatever you want."

As I sifted through Vicki's things, I realized how many of Vicki's memories were *my* memories. I silently grieved for this loss as I folded the ivory embroidered tablecloth she and Bill had bought in Mexico.

I stroked Vicki's decorative pillows she herself had crafted for their home, remembering the love that had gone into the tiny stitches. Upon seeing her sea-foam green quilt, I remembered how excited Vicki had been when she used it to decorate her bedroom. Now these things, these memories, meant nothing to her. The gracefulness of her Dresden plate quilt that had once covered her marriage bed seemed to mock me. *How,* I wondered, *could Vicki walk away from nineteen years of marriage to a loving husband? How could she exchange her past for a stranger?*

Sifting through Vicki's memories was troubling, but more troubling was the process of sifting through my own memories.

Again I thought of the pain of our family's tragedy and remembered how I had almost allowed grief to destroy the pattern of my own life's quilt:

It had been Paul's and my first chance to get away from the Intensive Care Unit that had invaded our home following Laura's car accident.

That evening, as we sat in an open-air restaurant, Paul asked, "Would you have married me if you had known our only daughter would be so severely disabled?"

I felt the night breeze rearrange my curls as I thought through the events of our recent past. I thought of the ten months that Laura, our then two-year-old child, had spent in a coma. I thought of all the emotional suffering that had stitched itself into a shroud of grief. I thought of Laura's wheelchair and life-support systems. "No," I finally whispered, willing to throw away the past in exchange for relief from my pain.

Paul stared at his grilled snapper, unable to look at me.

"I'm sorry," I said, "I love you, but I would have done anything to prevent Laura from being hurt, even if that meant never meeting you."

Now, five years later, as I looked at the remains of Vicki's discarded memories, I changed my mind about my answer to Paul's question. My memories, even those that were painful, were now precious to me.

Other memories began playing through my mind like bright ribbons of color. *I remembered the early-marriage water fights we'd splashed through our tiny lime-green apartment. I thought of the day Paul had almost squeezed off my fingers as I birthed our son. I thought about how hard Paul had worked to build our cedar fence so baby Laura and then Jimmy could toddle about the backyard of our first home.*

Yes, some of our memories were dark. But as I evaluated them, I realized how even they enriched the quilted pattern they helped to create.

Later that night, I reached for Paul's hand as we sat together on the sofa. "I'm sorry I told you I wouldn't have married you if I had known our daughter would one day be severely disabled."

Paul's blue eyes met mine.

I squeezed his hand. "I'm glad I married you. Despite what we've been through, we've been through it together, and I wouldn't change that for anything."

I snuggled closer to my husband, glad I had someone committed to making heirloom memories with me as long as the Lord would allow. And despite all our obstacles, we not only had each other, we had God, and we would overcome. With things in fresher perspective, I would cherish every patchworked moment of the crazy quilt that had become our lives.

The End

About Linda Evans Shepherd

Linda, the 1997 Colorado Christian author of the year, is the author of eight books including *Encouraging Hands, Encouraging Hearts* (Servant) and *Share Jesus without Fear* with Bill Fay (Broadman & Holman) and is a member of the National Speakers Association. She has been married for twenty years and has two children.

Linda makes her audiences laugh and cry as she shares her own stories. She reminds us that *Faith Never Shrinks in Hot Water* and *God Wants Spiritual Fruit Not Religious Nuts* and teaches us *How to Make Time* for our friends, family, and a relationship with God. She may be available for your next retreat or special event.

To check Linda's availability and fees go online to: http://www.sheppro.com or call Speak Up Speaker Services at (888) 870-7719 or CLASServices at (800) 433-6633.

Do you have a story of romance, faith, love, or hope to tell for a future book? If so, please send it to Linda at:

Heart-Stirring Stories
Attn: Linda Evans Shepherd
P.O. Box 7562
Longmont, CO 80501

or E-mail (paste into the text of your E-mail to Linda at): Lswrites@aol.com

For editorial guidelines, check Linda's web page at http://www.sheppro.com, or send a self-addressed-stamped-envelope to the address listed above.

◆◆◆

Permissions

"A Wife's Greatest Gift" was taken from *How to Become a Sweet Old Lady Instead of a Grumpy Old Grouch* by Marilynn Carlson. © 1996 by Marilynn Carlson Webber. Used by permission of Zondervan Publishing House.

"True Love Is Blind(folded)" by Liz Curtis Higgs, first appeared in the January/February 1996 issue of *Today's Christian Woman.*

"One of These Days" written by Vince Matthews, © 1967 Songs of PolyGram International, Inc. Copyright renewed. Used by permission. All rights reserved.

"The Big Squeeze" by Paul Kortepeter was reprinted from *Marriage Partnership* (Summer/1996).

"The Gift of Honor" was reprinted from *The Gift of Family, A Legacy of Love,* © 1991 Naomi Rhode, published by Thomas Nelson, Inc.

"The Unexpected Messenger" was reprinted from *Whispers from Heaven* by Dayle Allen Shockley. © 1994 by Pacific Press Publishing Association.

"Memory Quilt" was reprinted from *Faith Never Shrinks in Hot Water* © 1996 Linda E. Shepherd. Published by Pacific Press Publishing Association.

Contributors

I wish to thank the following people who graciously shared their lives with us:

Charlotte Adelsperger is a speaker and the author of two books and numerous articles and poems. Her credits include *Decision, Focus on the Family Clubhouse, Pray,* and *A Second Chicken Soup for the Woman's Soul.* You may contact her at 11629 Riley, Overland Park, KS 66210 or 913-345-1678.

Beverly J. Anderson is a freelance writer. She serves as facilitator for the Central Placer Caring Connection, networking churches to help needy people and leads a church cell group. She chairs a chapter of the Neuropathy Association for people suffering with peripheral neuropathy. Her contact address is bja@foothill.net.

Randolph Ed Arrington, retired railroad mechanic, enjoys writing poetry as a hobby. He wrote his poem, "Our Love Lingers On," in memory of his beloved wife, the late Lila Arrington. They had been married almost sixty years at the time of her death in 1995.

Marlene Bagnull and her husband, Paul, have been married thirty-five years and are the parents of three grown children. Marlene directs the Greater Philadelphia and Colorado Christian Writers' Conferences and gives writing seminars around the country. She is the author of six books. You can visit her web site at: http://nancepub.com/cwf/.

Vickey Banks is a happily married wife, mother, and inspirational speaker with CLASServices, Inc. She is also a freelance writer and author of the upcoming book, *Love Letters to My Baby.* You may contact Vickey at 405-728-2305 or online at vbinokc@aol.com.

Nancy Bayless is a seasoned writer and speaker. Her articles have appeared in books and major Christian magazines, including *Guideposts, Decision, Moody,* and others.

She is active in the San Diego County Christian Writers' Guild and received that organization's Writer of the Year award in 1993.

Ellen Bergh, speaker, and writer, and group leader, coaches reluctant writers to answer their call. She owns Mastermedia Publishing and oversaw the High Desert Christian Writers Guild's first book *Water from the Rock* in 1998. Contact her at mastermedia@hughes.net.

Barbara Loftus Boswell is a part-time registered nurse and full-time homemaker, living in Aston, Pennsylvania. This marks her first publication, for which she thanks God joyfully! She fully recommends the Christian Connections website at www.christian.email.net, through which she met her husband, Brian. You may contact her at Bx2Boswell@aol.com.

Debbie Brockett has been writing for the Colorado-based magazine, *The Testimony,* for five years. Her popular monthly column, "The Trumpet Vine," encourages Christians in their daily walks with the Lord. She is one of the founders of the Western Slope Christian Writers' Association and can be reached at DABrockett@aol.com.

Lenae Bulthuis is the author of two devotional books for children. As a speaker and writer, she dedicates herself to helping others improve their prayer life and communication with God. She and her husband Michael have three daughters, Elizabeth, Stephanie, and Melanie. She can be reached at lenae@willmar.com.

Georgia E. Burkett is a grandmother and great-grandmother. She clowns occasionally for children's programs and sings with a group of "over fifty-fivers" who refuse to grow old, for nursing homes, senior centers, and for various churches. Her E-mail address is georgiab2@juno.com.

Dianne E. Butts a freelance writer, has seen more than seventy-five publications of her work in magazines such as *Virtue, Focus on the Family, and Discipleship*

Journal. She and her husband, Hal, ride with the Christian Motorcyclists' Association. They live with their dog, Profile, in Lamar, Colorado. Contact her at dbwrites@juno.com.

Sue Cameron's passion is writing and speaking about issues related to biblical sexuality. She also enjoys worship dance, drama, serving at Christian writers' conferences, and her husband, Craig, who is an orthopedic oncologist. They have four children and a new daughter-in-law. You can reach Sue at smcameron@juno.com.

Denise Hawkins Camp, a freelance writer, lives with her family in Tennessee.

Beverly Caruso and her husband Pete, have pioneered and pastored two churches and ministered in forty countries. She has authored several books including *Developing Godly Character in Children,* and *Around the World—365 Faith Builders from 90 Countries.* She has trained writers on three continents. She can be reached at Caruso@xc.org.

Sandy Cathcart is an author, speaker, musician/singer who shares a message of encouragement for believers to put feet to their faith. Contact her at 341 Flounce Rock Rd., Prospect, OR 97536; 541-560-2367; or online at 75222.3643@compuserve.com.

Jan Coleman: Her partner, Carl, urged Jan Coleman to retire from a public relations job and pursue her passion of writing. With prayer and Carl's inspiration, she's written for publications like *Virtue, Mature Living, Young Miss,* and authored television documentaries for a worldwide ministry. Contact her at Jwriter@foothill.net.

Pamela F. Dowd has stories in two other books, *Why Fret That God Stuff?* and *Seasons of a Woman's Heart.* Her articles have appeared in *Christian Parenting Today, Pray!,* and *Evangelizing Today's Child.* She writes greeting cards for Dayspring and Celebration Greetings and is a Warner Press Master Writer. Contact her at dowpub@juno.com.

Bill Farrel is a senior pastor in San Diego, California. He and his wife Pam are the coauthors of several books, including *Pure Pleasure: Making Your Marriage a Great Affair* (coauthored with Jim and Sally Conway), *Marriage in the Whirlwind: Seven Skills for Couples Who Can't Slow Down* (IVP), and *Love to Love You* (Harvest House). He and Pam are marriage conference speakers and popular media guests.

Pam Farrel is married to Bill and has coauthored the books mentioned above. She is the director of women at their church in San Diego. Pam has also written books that include *Woman of Influence: Ten Traits of Those Who want to Make a Difference* and *A Woman God Can Use*. Pam writes for a number of magazines and is the mother of three active boys. E-mail Pam and Bill at mliving@webcc.com.

Karl J. Forehand is pastor of a local church in Stella, Nebraska. He sees writing as his second career and his third love, after his Lord and his family.

Jo Franz speaks at banquets, churches, retreats, and conferences around the country, weaving into each presentation songs from her CDs. She also does television and radio interviews. Her stories appear in a number of anthologies and magazines, and Jo is a member of CLASS. You may contact her at Jofranz@aol.com.

Donald Haines is a retired registered nurse who, except for military service, has lived his entire life in Carroll County, Maryland. He's been married to Sheila for forty-one years and has three sons and nine grandchildren. He teaches adult Sunday school and is a deacon at Liberty Baptist Church in Lisbon, Maryland.

Bonnie Compton Hanson, writer, editor, artist, and poet, has authored several books, including a Gold Medallion finalist. Her lively family includes husband Don, children, grandchildren, and assorted pets. You may reach Bonnie at 3330 S. Lowell St., Santa Ana, CA 92707, call at 714-751-7824, or E-mail her at bonnieh1@worldnet.att.net.

Voni K. Harris is the mother of a two-and-a-half-year-old spitfire named Leah, and the wife of a man of integrity named Rich. They make their home in southern Indiana. Some of the incidents in "The Wedding" actually happened, but Voni isn't saying which ones.

Laurie Heron is a freelance writer and editor. She is also the mother of Sydni, five, Xavier, three, and Jedediah, one. She can be contacted at Laurieheron@yahoo.com.

Heidi S. Hess is senior editor at Servant Publications. Her writing credits include *Let Nothing Trouble You* (Charis Books), *Quiet Moments with Oswald Chambers* (Vine Books), and "The Ladder Test" in *Love Adds a Little Chocolate* (Time Warner). Heidi and Craig Saxton were married in July 1999.

Liz Curtis Higgs is the best-selling author of five children's books and six humorous books for women, including *Only Angels Can Wing It* and *Help! I'm Laughing and I Can't Get Up.* A veteran of more than thirteen hundred presentations, Liz helps audiences learn how to lighten up with laughter. Her newest book, *Mixed Signals,* is a fun inspirational romance novel from Multnomah Publishers. For a copy of her free newsletter, *The Laughing Heart,* call 1-800-762-6565.

Nancy Hoag is a wife, mother, and grandmother with nearly eight hundred published articles and devotions to her credit. In addition, she is the author of three books including *Good Morning! Isn't It a Fabulous Day!* and *Storms Pass, So Hang On!* (both with Beacon Hill Press of Kansas City). Nancy is also a frequent speaker and teacher at writers' conferences and women's retreats.

Maxine Holmgren has had articles printed in magazines and has written weekly newspaper columns. She has been an announcer for a Christian radio station and enjoys speaking at women's meetings. Maxine is a CLASS graduate and a certified personality trainer. She conducts programs entitled *Find the Pizzazz in Your Personality.*

Jan Johnson is the author of ten books, including *Living a Purpose-Full Life* and *Enjoying the Presence of God.* She also enjoys speaking at retreats, hoping to create within people a burning desire to know God. You may contact her at JanJohnson@compuserve.com.

Dr. Linda Karges-Bone is a professor in the School of Education at Charleston Southern University. The author of twenty books and hundreds of articles and short stories, Dr. Bone is also the host of the radio program, "Prayerful Parenting." She has been married for twenty years to Gary Bone. They have two daughters and reside in Summerville, South Carolina.

Nancy Kennedy, known for her humor, is author of such books as *Help!, I'm Being Intimidated by the Proverbs 31 Woman, Mom on the Run,* and *Honey They're Playing Our Song* (Multnomah.) Her latest book is about the prayers God always answers (WaterBrook Press, Oct. 1999 release).

Carol Kent is an author and the founder and president of "Speak Up with Confidence" seminars, a ministry committed to helping Christians develop their communication skills. A member of the National Speakers' Association, Carol is scheduled more than a year in advance for keynote addresses at conferences and retreats. You can contact Carol at Speakupinc@aol.com or call her at 810-982-0898.

Carmen Leal-Pock is an author, speaker, and singer, often featured throughout the United States in church, business, and non-profit settings. She is the author of *Faces of Huntington's* and speaks about Huntington's disease and other topics that allow her to share her inspiring testimony. Carmen may be reached at promo@digital.net.

Marita Littauer is a professional speaker with more than twenty years experience. She is the author of nine books including *Personality Puzzle* and *Come As You Are* and is president of CLASServices Inc., an organization that provides resources, training, and promotion for speakers and authors. Contact her at P.O. Box 66810, Albuquerque, NM 87193, 800-433-6633, or www.classervices.com.

Dave Mattingly has been writing for magazines, newspapers, and websites for seven years. He's been happily married to his wonderful wife, Linda, for ten years, and has been blessed with a brilliant son, Seth. You may contact him at mattingly@bigfoot.com.

Donna McDonnall is a freelance Christian writer living in Lamar, Colorado. She and her husband Bruce have two children in college and one on the mission field. Donna has had several articles and devotionals published. She was selected as the 1998 Colorado School Nurse of the Year.

Martha McNatt, writer and watercolor artist, author of two books, *Feeding the Flock,* a cookbook for church kitchens, and *A Heritage Revisited,* which traces the history of one church congregation from 1867 to 1987. She is also a contributing editor for *Grandmother Earth's Healthy and Wise Cookbook* (1997) and *Angels, Messengers of Love and Grace* (1997). She is the mother of two, grandmother of four, and wife of Lynn, musician and teacher.

Julie Moran Medearis lives in Longmont, Colorado. She is a wife and a mother of three children for her full-time career. In her spare time, she enjoys running a small web design business out of her home. (She designs and maintains Linda's web page.) You may contact her at mnc@mncweb.com.

Kathy Collard Miller is a wife, mother of two adult children, author of more than forty books, and a speaker. Her best-selling book is *God's Vitamin "C" for the Spirit.* She has spoken in over twenty-two states and three foreign countries. Contact her at PO Box 1058, Placentis, CA 92871, 714-933-2654, or Kathyspeak@aol.com.

DiAnn G. Mills lives in Houston, Texas, with her husband. They are the parents of four grown sons and are active members of Metropolitan Baptist Church. Her writing credits include two books published by Heartsong, short stories, articles, and devotionals. Contact her at 14410 Dracaena Court, Houston, TX, 77070 or millsdg@flash.net.

Lynda Munfrada, founding member of Western Slope Christian Writers' Association, lives in Grand Junction, Colorado, with her husband and three beautiful children. She has had articles and poems published in local papers and is currently working on a devotional poem book and a novel. You may contact her at MAMACOW2@aol.com.

Connie Neal is the author of *Dancing in the Arms of God* and *Holding On to Heaven While Your Husband Goes through Hell.* She has coauthored books with Dave and Jan Dravecky, Steve Arterburn, and Bill and Lyndi McCartney. In 1998 Connie was the guest speaker at fifteen Women of Faith Bring Back the Joy conferences. Contact her through Susan Yates at 714-285-9540.

William R. Nesbitt Jr., M.D., graduated from Duke University with a B.S. in medicine and an M.D. He has been in private practice (family medicine with a sub-specialty in psychiatry) for twenty years and on the faculty of the University of California (Davis) Medical School for five years. He is also a lecturer, counselor, teacher, and freelance writer.

Rose Hampton Newton's life and stories are laced with the richness of faith in the lives of those whom the Lord has graciously placed in her path. This secretary-teacher-writer, and jenny-come-lately to faith and writing is awed and delighted to know him.

Jan Northington is a freelance writer and conference speaker, trained and promoted through CLASS (Christian Leaders and Speakers Services). She is the author of the book *Separated and Waiting* (Thomas Nelson, 1994) and has written numerous articles for the Christian marketplace. Jan resides on the central coast of California with her husband and four children. Contact her at 2130 Sombrero Dr., Los Osos, CA 93402, 805-528-2522, or apleaday4u@aol.com.

D. J. Note is a member of Oregon Christian Writers', Moms in Touch Int'l., is a regular contributor to *Cascade Horseman* magazine, and has articles in national publications. Her love of God, family, and country life inspire her writing. Contact her at djnote@juno.com.

Karen O'Connor is a sought-after speaker and author of thirty-five books, including *Basket of Blessings* and *Squeeze the Moment*. She is a member of CLASS Speakers and the American Society of Journalists and Authors. Karen was awarded the 1997 Writer of the Year Award from the San Diego Christian Writers' Guild.

Susan Titus Osborn is a contributing editor of *The Christian Communicator* and an adjunct professor at Hope International University. She has authored nineteen books and numerous articles. She has taught at more than 110 writers conferences across the U.S. Contact Susan at 3133 Puente Street, Fullerton, CA 92835, 714-990-1532, or Susanosb@aol.com. Website: christiancommunicator.com.

Dr. Terry Paulson of Agoura Hills, California, is the 1998/99 President of the National Speakers' Association and author of *Meditations for the Road Warrior* and *50 Tips for Speaking Like a Pro*. He helps leaders and teams make change work. Contact him at 818-991-5110 or DrTerryP@aol.com or visit his website at http://www.changecentral.com.

S. F. Peacock lives in Lamar, Colorado, writes a weekly personal/humor column, "Peacock Tales," and may be contacted at peacfam@ria.net.

Naomi Rhode, RDH, CSP, CPAE, is past president of the National Speakers' Association and recent recipient of the Cavett Award, the organization's highest honor. Naomi is known for her motivational, dynamic speaking to both healthcare and general audiences. She is co-owner and vice president of SmartPractice, a marketing and manufacturing company that provides products and services to the healthcare industry worldwide. Naomi is the author of two inspirational gift books, *The Gift of Family—A Legacy of Love* and *More Beautiful Than Diamonds—The Gift of Friendship*. Naomi is also copublisher of PracticeSmart, a newsletter for dental professionals.

Orallee Zaleine Robinson, a freelance writer and reporter, lives in Las Animas, Colorado, with her husband Tom of twelve years and four children. She is credited with several newspaper and magazine articles, and most recently, a book entitled *Deadly Dose: America's Vaccine Victims.*

Jane A. Rubietta, a pastor's wife and mother of three, is the author of *Quiet Places: A Woman's Guide to Personal Retreat* (Bethany House, 1997), *Still Waters* (1999), and nearly sixty articles, and speaks widely at women's events. Jane and Rich met on an escalator and have been going up ever since.

Suzy Ryan lives in southern California with her husband and three small children. Her articles have appeared in *Bounce Back Too, Today's Christian Woman, Woman's World, The American Enterprise,* and various newspapers. Contact her at KenSuzy@aol.com.

Carolyn R. Scheidies has six books released by Heartsong Presents, with four books due out soon from Mountainview Publishing. In the last two years, two of her books have made the Heartsong top ten historical list. She is a member of Romance Writers of America and the Published Author's Network.

Sheila Seifert teaches article writing at the University of Colorado at Denver, is the editor of *Gristmill,* and speaks at writing conferences. She is the cofounder of the Colorado Writers Fellowship, an organization that supports Christian writers through networking, monthly meetings, and contests. She can be reached at seifert@rmi.net.

Maggie Mae Sharp, 1996 National Lady Cowboy Poet, also speaks across the county on issues of women's self-esteem. The author of *The Huntress, Searching for Mr. Right,* and five albums of original poetry, she is also a rancher, a member of the Pikes Peaks Arts Council, and holds a board membership with the Black Forest Arts Guild. Contact her at huntress@iex.net.

Dayle Allen Shockley is an inspirational speaker and the author of *Whispers from Heaven* and *Silver Linings* (Pacific Press.) Her work has appeared in numerous periodicals, including *Guideposts, Focus on the Family, Moody, Houston Chronicle,* and *Catholic Digest.* She is the founder of Writers Anonymous and conducts writing workshops around the country.

Doris Smalling is a retired English teacher, a published poet, and author. She received the Valley Forge Freedoms Foundation Award for her play, *A Century of Americana,* and the same organization's Poetry Award for her poem, "I Touched the Hand of America." She is a national speaker for Stonecroft Ministries.

Steven G. Standerfer a former journalist who worked for newspapers in California and Nevada, is director of public relations at Antelope Valley College. He and his wife Carolyn have three children. They reside in Quartz Hill, California.

Rhonda Wheeler Stock lives in Kansas with her husband, Rick, their four children, a flock of parakeets, and one blue Beta fish. Rhonda loves thrift stores and garage sales, and wishes she had more time (and money) for both. If you'd like Rhonda to speak to your church, conference, or youth group, contact her at (913) 492-9607, or via E-mail at: RondaWS@juno.com.

Ronica Stromberg has worked as a newspaper reporter, a marketing assistant, and an editor for an educational corporation. She now works at home, caring for her sons and writing freelance. Her stories have appeared in four books and numerous newspapers and magazines.

Andy Terry is a career air force noncommissioned officer and pastor, and has spent his entire adult life serving both "God and Country." This dual vocation has taken him around the globe, ministering under unique situations. He's most recently pastored New Horizons Church in Alexandria, Virginia. You may contact him at pneumos@aol.com.

Nanette Thorsen-Snipes, a freelance writer for eighteen years, has had more than 250 articles, columns, stories, and devotions in at least thirty different publications. Among them are: *Honor Books, Publications International, Inc., The Christian Reader, Georgia Magazine, Breakaway, Accent on Living, Home Life, Experiencing God Magazine, Woman's Touch, Power for Living,* and *The Upper Room.*

Bobbie Wilkinson is a freelance writer, artist, musician, and songwriter, whose proudest accomplishments are her three grown daughters. She lives with her husband in a renovated barn in the northern Virginia countryside, where her favorite pastime is appreciating the beauty that surrounds her.

Connie Bertelsen Young, homemaker and freelance writer, has written the column "Valley Gal" for two California, San Joaquin Valley, newspapers for six years. Her work has also been published by Augsburg Publishing House in Minneapolis and Word Action Publishing in Kansas City, Missouri. You may contact her at VALEGAL@juno.com.

Diane Zuidema has been married to Lance for fifteen years. They have two sons, Lucas and Lane. Diane is a loan officer, working with farmers in Minnesota. Her address is 19332 30th St SW, Blomkest, MN 56216. She and Lenae Bulthuis speak to women's groups and collaborate on writing projects.